MUSHROOMS

The new compact study guide and identifier

David Pegler & Brian Spooner

CHARTWELL
BOOKS, INC.

A QUINTET BOOK

Published by Chartwell Books
A Division of Book Sales, Inc.
110 Enterprise Avenue
Secaucus, New Jersey 07094

This edition produced for sale
in the U.S.A., its territories
and dependencies only.

ISBN 0-7858-0048-4

This book was designed and produced by
Quintet Publishing Limited
6 Blundell Street
London N7 9BH

Creative Director: Richard Dewing
Designer: Bob Mathias
Project Editor: Helen Denholm
Editor: Tucker Slingsby

With thanks to Richard Fortey for checking text

Photographs courtesy of: A. W. Brand, Gordon Dickson, Margaret Holden, Thomas Laessøe, Nick Legon, Alan Outen, David Pegler, Jens H. Peterson and Brian Spooner

Typeset in Great Britain by
Central Southern Typesetters, Eastbourne
Manufactured in Singapore by Eray Scan Pte. Ltd
Printed in Singapore by Star Standard Industries Pte. Ltd

A number of mushrooms are poisonous and some are deadly poisonous. It is therefore vitally important that you are absolutely sure of the identity of any mushroom before eating it. It is always best to consult an expert. If there is any doubt at all about the identity of a mushroom, do not eat it.

The publisher and authors of this book have made every effort to ensure that the information contained in it is accurate and factually correct. Any information regarding the edibility of any mushroom is provided for guidance only. The publisher and authors can not accept legal responsibility for any errors or omissions or for any actions taken arising from the information contained in this book.

CONTENTS

Key to Symbols 6

Glossary 7

Directory of fungi 8

Index of common names 80

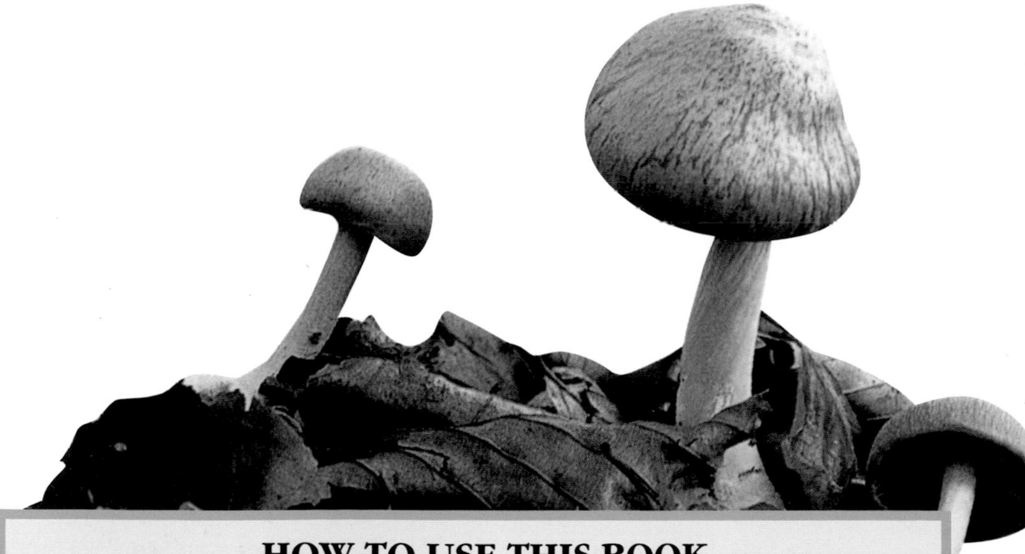

HOW TO USE THIS BOOK

The species are arranged alphabetically by Latin name, with key symbols to aid identification. Each entry includes a colour photograph and detailed description plus notes on visually similar species. Also included are at-a-glance symbols to indicate the season – spring, summer, autumn and winter – when the fungus is likely to be found, its edibility – edible, inedible, poisonous, or if its edibility is unknown – and the habitat in which you are likely to find it – in woodlands, grasslands and open spaces, on trees or woody stumps, in bogs and marshland, on burnt ground, on dung or enriched soil, or growing on other fungi. Such detailed information should avoid confusion.

EDIBLE AND POISONOUS FUNGI

Edible species

Fleshy fungi have been eaten since ancient times and in many countries, especially in Eastern Europe, the gathering of wild mushrooms is carried out on a commercial scale. Fungi, in addition to adding flavour and texture to a host of recipes, contain more digestible protein than any green vegetable, are high in carbohydrates, fibre and vitamins, and low in fat.

Wild edible mushrooms should be picked carefully, avoiding any old or insect-infested specimens. It is recommended not to mix species in any one dish and to be absolutely certain of the identification. If in doubt – don't eat it!

Poisonous fungi

Some wild fungi are deadly poisonous even in quite small amounts. On returning from a collecting trip, always remember to wash your hands. There are a number of different types of fungus poisoning, and symptoms can vary from abdominal pains, nausea, vomiting and intense thirst occurring within 8–15 hours when the deadly poisonous fungus – the Death Cap – has been eaten for instance, to a violent reaction occurring within 10 minutes, when the otherwise edible Common Ink-cap is eaten accompanied by alcohol. Some species can cause drowsiness, and hallucinations which may lead to coma.

There are also a large number of species which, while not deadly poisonous, can cause severe stomach upsets.

Avoid eating all the species not clearly marked as edible within this guide, and take special note where cooking or the avoidance of alcohol are necessary to ensure edibility. Never eat a species that you have not definitely identified as edible.

REMEMBER

- *Learn to recognize the deadly species, especially the Death Cap – and then avoid them*
- *Make certain of identification, and do not mix species*
- *Use only fresh clean specimens, and ensure they are properly cooked*
- *If trying a known edible species new to you, only sample a small quantity*
- *If you suffer the effects of poisoning, even mildly, seek medical advice immediately* ***especially*** *if there is a delay in symptoms*

MAJOR GROUPS OF FUNGI

Without going into the details of classification there are nine groups of fungi that the collector will need to recognize.

Chanterelles

This small group contains one of the best-known edible fungi. It includes short-lived fleshy fungi which initially resemble mushrooms and toadstools, however chanterelles *(below)* have thick, branching ridges with blunt edges unlike mushrooms which have radiating gills on the underside of the cap.

Mushrooms and Toadstools

These form the majority of species illustrated in this book, and are the most frequently observed being commonly found in woodlands in the autumn *(below left)*. There is no scientific distinction between a mushroom and a toadstool, and the belief that the former is edible and latter poisonous has many exceptions. This group includes the commercial edible mushrooms as well as the deadly poisonous *Amanita* species.

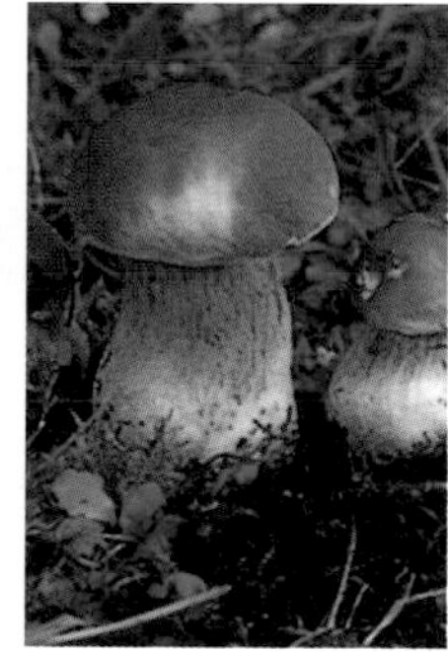

Boletes

Related to the mushrooms and toadstools, boletes *(above right)* are distinctive in producing spores not on radiating gills but inside a series of closely compacted vertical tubes, each opening by a basal pore on the underside of the cap. Ceps are among the most highly prized of edible fungi.

Club fungi

Club fungi *(below)* are, for the most part, soft and fleshy fungi. They are often highly coloured. The club fungi resemble erect

simple clubs, either solitary or clustered, or may be highly branched. Although most species are harmless, they are rarely recommended for eating, and a few will cause serious stomach upsets.

Bracket fungi

Species of this large group *(below left)* are found mainly on dead or living wood. They are long-lived, have a tough texture and develop slowly. Many brackets are serious pathogens of forest and plantation trees, while others, such as Dry Rot Fungus can attack household woodwork.

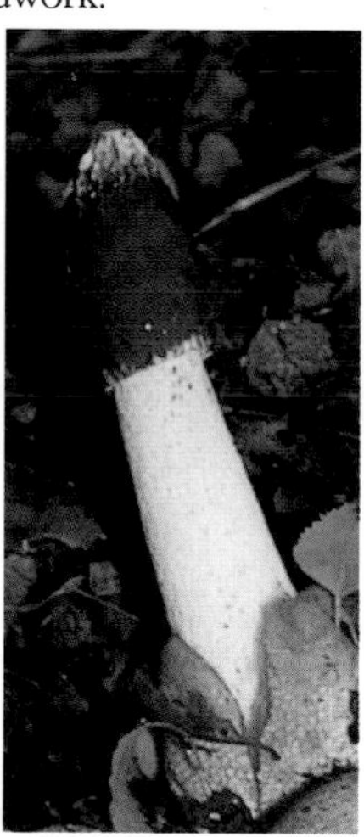

Stinkhorns

Stinkhorns *(above right)* form a soft, gelatinous "egg-stage" which eventually ruptures to release either a tall, spongy stem, or a netlike structure that expands rapidly and bears a slimy region containing spores; the slime having a strong and unpleasant smell.

Jelly fungi

This group is aptly named, as the species often resemble gelatinous blobs. In dry conditions these fungi may dry to a fine film on woody substrate, becoming reconstituted in wet weather *(below left)*. Few species are regarded as edible, although one or two are used for their texture in Chinese cuisine.

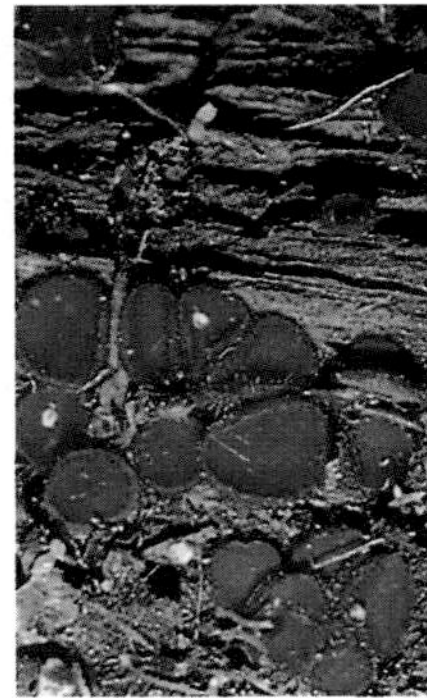

Cup fungi and flask fungi

Cup fungi are colourful and easily recognizable, producing a cup- or disc-shaped structure lined inside with a spore-producing layer *(above right)*. Flask fungi appear rounded or bottle-shaped.

Puffballs and relatives

Puffballs *(below)*, earthstars, bird's nest fungi and earthballs have spores that are either released in clouds through a pore, or the fruitbody breaks down due to weathering. All true puffballs are edible when young.

KEY TO SYMBOLS

EDIBLE

INEDIBLE

DEADLY POISONOUS

POISONOUS

EDIBILITY UNKNOWN

SPRING

SUMMER

AUTUMN

WINTER

On the ground in woodlands or associated with trees

On the ground in grasslands or open spaces

On trees, stumps or woody debris

In wet situations, such as bogs and marshlands

On burnt ground or on burnt wood

On dung or enriched soil

On other fungi

GLOSSARY

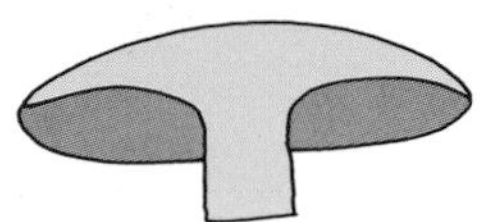

ADNATE (of gills, tubes) – broadly attached to stem apex

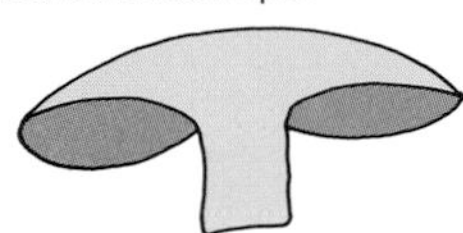

ADNEXED (of gills, tubes) – narrowly attached to stem apex

CAMPANULATE (of cap) – bell-shaped

CAPITATE – with a swollen apex

CONVEX (of cap) – broadly rounded upwards in outline

CRENULATE – minutely toothed

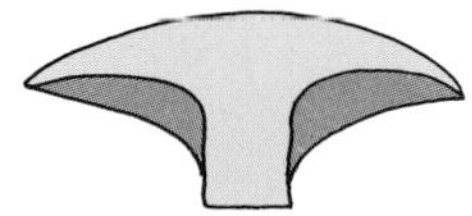

DECURRENT (of gills, tubes) – broad attachment which extends down the stem

EXPANDED (of cap) – opening fully at maturity

FERTILE SURFACE – spore-producing surface

FIBRIL – a small fibre

FIBRILLOSE – bearing fibrils

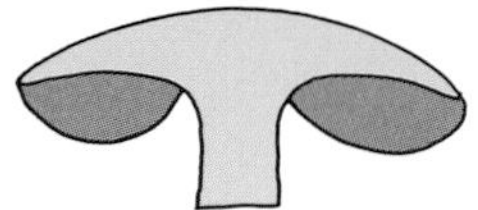

FREE (of gills, tubes) – not reaching the stem apex

FRUITBODY – the structure which supports the spore-producing layers of a fungus, visible to the naked eye (eg mushroom)

MYCELIUM – a mass of hyphae, usually embedded within the substrate

OBTUSE (of cap margin) – thick and rounded

PAPILLATE (of cap) – with a prominent central projection

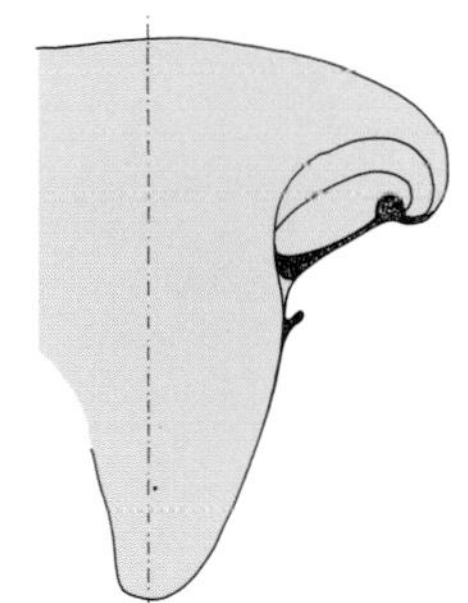

PARTIAL VEIL – a protective layer of certain young mushroom fruitbodies

PILEUS – the cap of a mushroom or bracket-fungus

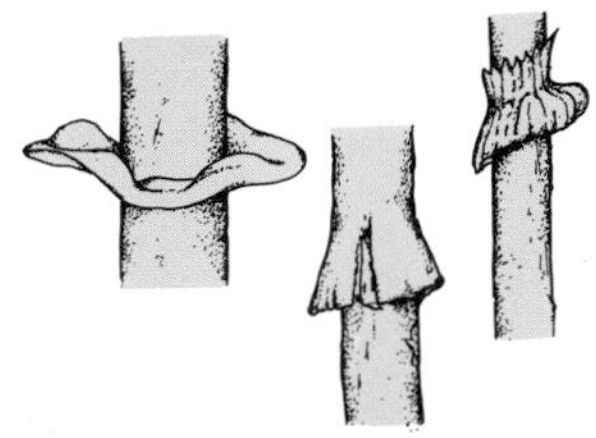

RING – the membranous remains of the partial veil, attached to the stem

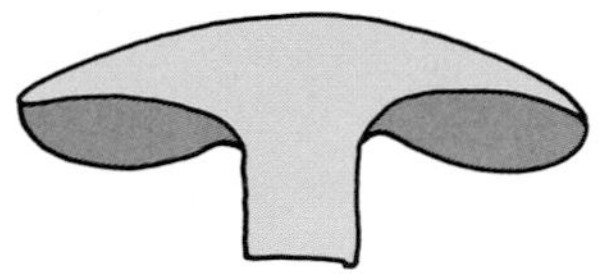

SINUATE (of gills, tubes) – curving upwards just before the point of attachment to the stem

SPORE – the reproductive, one-celled unit of a fungus

STIPE – the stem of a mushroom

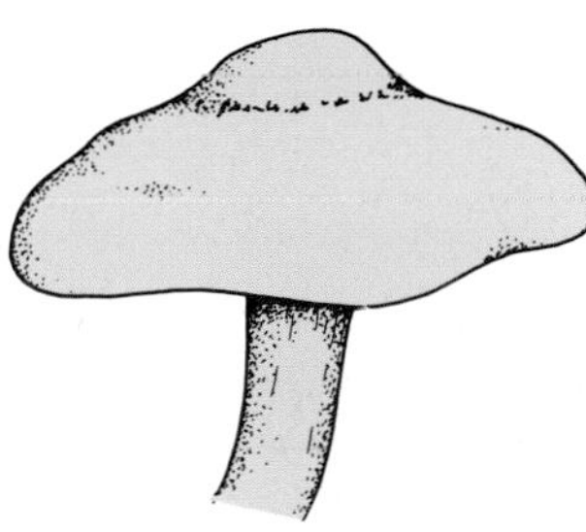

UMBONATE (of cap) – having a raised area (or umbo) at the centre

VEIL – a protective layer covering the button-stage of mushrooms

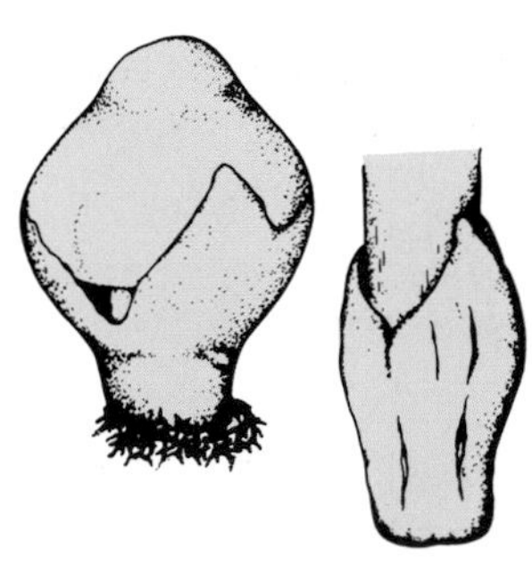

VOLVA – a cup-like structure at the stem base, derived from the veil

AGARICUS ARVENSIS

Horse Mushroom

A common, grassland true mushroom, which discolours yellowish on bruising.

Cap 2¾–6 in/7–15 cm in diameter, convex, expanding, white, bruising pale yellow when the surface is rubbed, smooth to slightly scaly, with remnants of veil hanging from the margin. *Gills* free, greyish darkening to chocolate-brown, broad and crowded. *Stem* 2¾–4¾ × ⅜–¾ in/7–12 × 1–2 cm, cylindrical, smooth, white, bruising yellow, bearing a white, membranous, thick ring on the upper region. *Flesh* thick, white, with a smell of bitter almonds. *Spore deposit* blackish brown. *Habitat* pastureland. *Similar species* the poisonous *A. xanthodermus*, (page 10) has a large ring, and an unpleasant smell, and the stem base discolours yellow. The edible *A. campestris* (page 9) does not bruise yellow. *Edibility* edible and good.

GROUP Mushrooms and Toadstools
FAMILY Mushroom and Lepiota (Agaricaceae)

SEASON 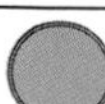 **EDIBILITY** 

HABITAT  On the ground in grassland or open spaces

AGARICUS AUGUSTUS

The Prince

One of the largest of the true mushrooms, with a yellowish brown, scaly cap, bruising deep yellow when rubbed.

Cap 4–8 in/10–20 cm in diameter, almost spherical then expanding, retaining flattened top, covered with small, tawny brown, fibrous scales in concentric rings on a white to yellowish background, bruising deep yellow. *Gills* free, pinkish to blackish brown, crowded. *Stem* 4–8 × ¾–1¼ in/10–20 × 2–3 cm, thicker towards the base, hollow, white, bruising yellow, smooth above the ring, soft-scaly below the ring. *Ring* large, membranous, white, attached towards the top of the stem. *Flesh* white, with a pleasant smell of bitter almonds. *Spore deposit* brownish black. *Habitat* on forest floor or in parks under deciduous trees. *Similar species* unlikely to be confused. *Edibility* excellent.

GROUP Mushrooms and Toadstools
FAMILY Mushroom and Lepiota (Agaricaceae)

SEASON  **EDIBILITY** 

HABITAT  On the ground in woodlands or associated with trees

AGARICUS CAMPESTRIS

Field Mushroom

The best-known mushroom, distinguished by the reddening flesh, and the small, simple ring on the stem.

Cap 1¼–3 in/3–8 cm in diameter, convex becoming almost flat, pure white or sometimes with greyish tints at the centre, dry, smooth or indistinctly scaly in old specimens. *Gills* free, bright pink becoming dark chocolate-brown, broad and crowded. *Stem* 1¼–2¼ × ⅜–⅝ in/3–6 × 1–1.5 cm, short and cylindrical or tapering at the base, white, smooth, bearing a small, thin ring which easily disappears on weathering. *Flesh* thick, white discolouring pinkish when broken open, with a pleasant smell. *Spore deposit* blackish brown. *Habitat* common, scattered in open grassland. *Similar species A. arvensis* (page 8) is larger and bruises yellow, and the Cultivated Mushroom (*A. bisporus*) has a much larger ring; both edible. *Edibility* good.

GROUP Mushrooms and Toadstools
FAMILY Mushroom and Lepiota (Agaricaceae)

SEASON 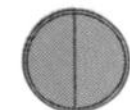 **EDIBILITY** 

HABITAT  On the ground in grassland or open spaces

AGARICUS SILVATICUS

Scaly Wood Mushroom

A true mushroom found in coniferous woods, and recognized by the dark brown scaly cap, pink to blackish brown gills, and a flesh that darkens to blood-red when broken open.

Cap 2¼–4 in/6–10 cm in diameter, strongly convex then flattening, with large, fibrous scales and a thin margin. *Gills* free, thin, broad and crowded, becoming darker with age. *Stem* 2¾–4 × ⅜–¾ in/7–10 × 1–2 cm, cylindrical, slightly swollen at the base, pale brown. *Flesh* firm and white, immediately discolouring. *Spore deposit* blackish brown. *Habitat* among conifer needles on woodland floor. *Similar species A. haemorrhoidarius* is larger and not confined to conifer woods, while *A. silvicola* is creamy white; both edible. *Edibility* edible but not recommended.

GROUP Mushrooms and Toadstools
FAMILY Mushroom and Lepiota (Agaricaceae)

SEASON  **EDIBILITY** 

HABITAT  On the ground in woodlands or associated with trees

AGARICUS XANTHODERMUS

Yellow-Staining Mushroom *or* Yellow-Foot Agaricus

A large and common, true mushroom, recognized by the bright yellow discoloration of the flesh at the stem base.

Cap 2¼–4¾ in/6–12 cm in diameter, strongly convex then gradually expanding to flat, white or perhaps with a pale greyish centre, dry, bruising bright yellow. *Gills* free, white becoming pinkish and finally dark chocolate-brown. *Stem* 2–4¾ × ⅜–¾ in/5–12 × 1–2 cm, cylindrical with a slightly swollen base, white, smooth, bruising yellow; very large, white, membranous ring on the upper region. *Flesh* white, soft, with an unpleasant carbolic odour. *Spore deposit* purplish brown. *Habitat* often under hedges or beside paths. *Similar species* the poisonous *A. placomyces* is very closely related but has small, sooty brown scales over the cap. *Edibility* **poisonous.**

GROUP Mushrooms and Toadstools
FAMILY Mushroom and Lepiota (Agaricaceae)

SEASON 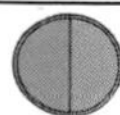 **EDIBILITY** 

HABITAT  On the ground in grassland or open spaces

AGROCYBE PRAECOX

Spring Agaric

A common springtime mushroom, with brown gills and a ring on the stem.

Cap 1¼–4 in/3–10 cm in diameter, broadly convex then becoming flattened, with a wavy margin, pale reddish brown, dry, smooth. *Gills* adnexed, whitish to cinnamon-brown, broad and crowded. *Stem* 2–4 × 3⁄16–⅝ in/5–10 × 0.5–1.5 cm, cylindrical, whitish, smooth, bearing a conspicuous membranous ring on the upper region. *Flesh* fairly thick, off-white, with an odour of damp flour. *Spore deposit* cinnamon-brown. *Habitat* often in scattered groups among grass and on bare soil. *Similar species A. semiorbicularis* is smaller, yellowish buff and lacks a ring on the stem; inedible. *Edibility* not recommended.

GROUP Mushrooms and Toadstools
FAMILY Bolbitius (Bolbitiaceae)

SEASON  **EDIBILITY** 

HABITAT  On the ground in grassland or open spaces

ALBATRELLUS OVINUS
Sheep Polypore

This polypore fungi grows on the ground, rather than on wood.

Cap 2¼–4 in/6–10 cm in diameter, strongly convex then flattened or depressed, often irregular, dry, white to yellowish, bruising brownish, smooth or with ill defined small scales, and a wavy margin. *Tubes* decurrent, short, 1⁄16 in/0.1–0.2 cm long, white; *pores* very small and difficult to see with the naked eye, white to lemon-yellow. *Stem* 1¼–2¼ × ⅜–¾ in/3–6 × 1–2 cm, central or excentric, curved, solid, hard, whitish. *Flesh* thick, white, with a fruity odour. *Spore deposit* white. *Habitat* among grass in open spruce forests, especially in mountainous areas. *Similar species A. confluens* is pale orange, with a white pore surface; edible. *Edibility* edible and good.

GROUP Bracket Fungi
FAMILY Hydnum (Hydnaceae)

SEASON 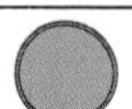 **EDIBILITY** 

HABITAT  On the ground in grassland or open spaces

ALEURIA AURANTIA
Orange Peel Fungus

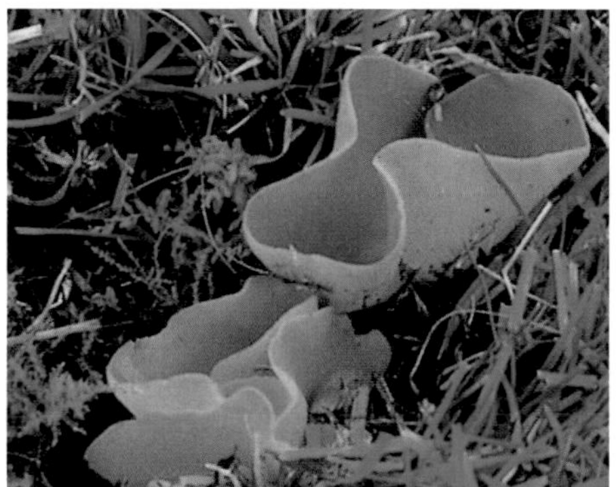

A large, distinctive species recognized by the bright orange, usually clustered, cup-shaped fruitbodies.

Fruitbody ¾–4 in/2–10 cm across, irregularly cup-shaped, often expanded and sometimes split at the margin, lacking a stalk. *Inner surface* bright orange, smooth. *Outer surface* whitish or very pale orange, minutely downy, especially near the margin. *Flesh* thin, fragile, whitish, without a distinctive smell. *Habitat* usually on bare soil or in open woods, gregarious and often clustered. *Similar species Melastiza chateri* is bright orange, but has smaller, less cup-shaped fruitbodies with short, brown hairs at the margin; inedible. *Edibility* edible but worthless.

GROUP Cup Fungi
FAMILY Eyelash Cup Fungi (Pyronemataceae)

SEASON 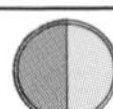 **EDIBILITY** 

HABITAT  On the ground in grassland or open spaces

AMANITA CITRINA

False Death Cap *or* Citron Amanita

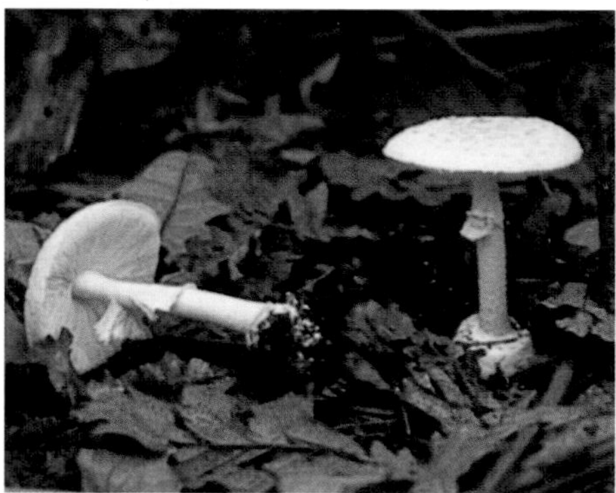

Recognized by the combination of a lemon-yellow or whitish cap with white scales, white gills, and stem with a ring and a very swollen, rimmed based.

Cap 1½–3 in/4–8 cm in diameter, convex with an incurved margin, smooth but with membranous white patches of the fragmenting veil. *Gills* free, broad, crowded. *Stem* 2¾–4¾ × ⅜–⅝ in/7–12 × 1–1.5 cm, abruptly swollen at the base, white, bearing a membranous ring near the apex and a volva which forms a prominent basal rim. *Flesh* white, thick, smelling of raw potatoes. *Spore deposit* white. *Habitat* solitary, in both pine and oak woods. *Similar species A. phalloides* (see p. 13) has a greeny bronze, streaky cap; deadly poisonous. *A. junquillea* has a ridged cap margin; poisonous. *Edibility* must be avoided owing to similarity to the Death Cap.

GROUP Mushrooms and Toadstools
FAMILY Amanita (Amanitaceae)

SEASON 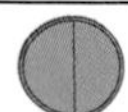 **EDIBILITY** 

HABITAT  On the ground in woodlands or associated with trees

AMANITA MUSCARIA

Fly Agaric

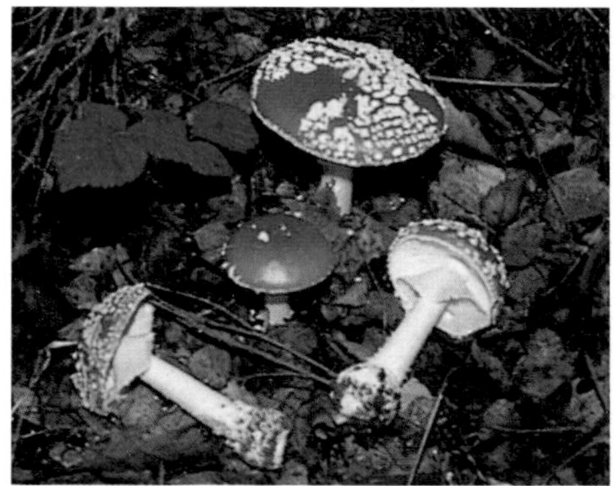

Perhaps the best-known wild mushroom, having a large, scarlet cap with small white scales.

Cap 2–9 in/5–25 cm in diameter, strongly rounded then expanding to flat and plate-like, moist and shiny, with concentric rings of small white scales which may become washed away by the rain. *Gills* free, white to pale yellow, broad and crowded. *Stem* 4–9 × ⅜–1 in/10–25 × 1–2.5 cm, tall, cylindrical with a swollen base, whitish, bearing small scales of veil in rings at the base. *Flesh* thick, white, yellowish under cap cuticle. *Spore deposit* white. *Habitat* in small groups, under pine or birch. *Similar species* the variety *regalis* is yellowish brown with yellow scales, and in North America, the variety *formosa* is orange-yellow; both poisonous. *Edibility* **poisonous** can cause delirium and coma.

GROUP Mushrooms and Toadstools
FAMILY Amanita (Amanitaceae)

SEASON  **EDIBILITY** 

HABITAT  On the ground in woodlands or associated with trees

AMANITA PHALLOIDES

Death Cap

Deadly poisonous, even in small amounts, always wash your hands after picking. Note the streaky, olive yellow cap, white gills, ring and sac-like volva on stem.

Cap 2¼–4¾ in/6–12 cm in diameter, convex, yellowish green, smooth and shiny. *Gills* free, white, broad, crowded. *Stem* 2¼–4 × ⅜–¾ in/6–10 × 1–2 cm, broader below, with a swollen base, white with zig-zag pattern; *ring* membranous, hanging downwards; *volva* white, membranous. *Flesh* white, with unpleasant, sickly smell. *Spore deposit* white. *Habitat* solitary, in woodlands, especially under oak trees. *Similar species* the edible true mushrooms (*Agaricus* species) can be confused but have gills which discolour from pink to blackish brown. *Edibility* **deadly poisonous.**

GROUP Mushrooms and Toadstools
FAMILY Amanita (Amanitaceae)

SEASON  **EDIBILITY** 

HABITAT  On the ground in woodlands or associated with trees

ARMILLARIA MELLEA

Honey Fungus

A fleshy mushroom recognized by the whitish gills and the ring on the stem.

Cap 1¼–4¾ in/3–12 cm in diameter, convex to flattened with a wavy margin, yellow-brown, with tiny, scattered dark brown scales, sticky when young and fresh. *Gills* shortly decurrent, whitish but developing reddish stains, crowded. *Stem* 2–6 × ⅜–¾ in/5–15 × 1–2 cm, cylindrical, soon hollow, whitish becoming rusty brown, fibrous, with a thick, cottony ring; the stem is attached at the base to thick, black, coarse threads which spread over the host plant. *Flesh* white, firm. *Spore deposit* white. *Habitat* on deciduous trees. *Similar species A. tabescens* lacks a ring on the stem, while *A. ostoyae* has a pinkish cap and attacks conifer trees. Edibility as for *A. mellea*. *Edibility* caps edible when young, can cause allergic reactions.

GROUP Mushrooms and Toadstools
FAMILY Tricholoma (Tricholomataceae)

SEASON  **EDIBILITY** 

HABITAT  On trees, stumps or woody debris

AURICULARIA AURICULA-JUDAE Jew's Ear *or* Tree Ear

A distinctive species recognized by the gel-tinous, ear-shaped fruitbodies growing on dead wood.

Fruitbody 1¼–4 in/3–10 cm across, irregularly cup-shaped or ear-shaped, reddish brown, gelatinous, drying hard; laterally attached without a stalk, the outer surface covered with short, greyish hairs. *Fertile surface* greyish brown, usually wrinkled or veined, otherwise smooth. *Flesh* thin, slightly translucent; no distinctive smell. *Spore deposit* white. *Habitat* on dead branches, especially of elder and elm, usually gregarious; common. *Similar species* unlikely to be confused with other species. *Edibility* edible.

GROUP Jelly Fungi
FAMILY Jew's Ear (Auriculariaceae)

SEASON  **EDIBILITY** 

HABITAT  On trees, stumps or woody debris

BOLETUS EDULIS
Cep or Penny Bun Boletus

A robust species recognized by the brown cap, pale stem with white network on the upper part, and white, unchanging flesh.

Cap 3–8 in/8–20 cm across, usually hemispherical, brown, slightly paler at the margin, smooth, dry or slightly sticky in moist weather. *Tubes* white or cream; *pores* whitish, small. *Flesh* whitish, not changing colour when cut. *Stem* 3–7 × 1½–2¾ in/8–18 × 4–7 cm, thickened below, whitish or pale brown, bearing in the upper part a network of white, raised lines. *Spore deposit* olive-brown. *Habitat* common in all types of woodland, mostly beech and oak, occasionally pine. *Similar species B. aestivalis* is very similar, but has a paler cap and a coarse network covering the whole length of the stem; edible. *Edibility* a good edible species, much sought after and used as a flavouring in soups.

GROUP Boletes
FAMILY Boletus (Boletaceae)

SEASON  **EDIBILITY** 

HABITAT  On the ground in woodlands or associated with trees

BOVISTA NIGRESCENS

Dusty Puffball

One of the common, small, white puffballs, characterized by the absence of any stalk-like base.

Fruitbody 1¼–2¼ in/3–6 cm in diameter, ball-shaped, pure white but with the outer layer progressively flaking away to leave a shiny, black inner layer exposed, and the apex breaking open in an irregular fashion to release the powdery spore-mass. *Flesh* white and firm, then purplish black and powdery. *Spore deposit* purplish black. *Habitat* common, on open grassland, at first attached at the base but eventually breaking away and rolling free. *Similar species B. plumbea* is smaller, with a greyish inner layer; edible. *Edibility* edible when young and while the flesh is still white.

GROUP Puffballs and Allies
FAMILY Puffball (Lycoperdaceae)

SEASON 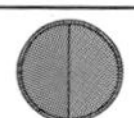 **EDIBILITY** 

HABITAT  On the ground in grassland or open spaces

CALOCERA VISCOSA

Jelly Antler Fungus *or* Yellow Tuning Fork

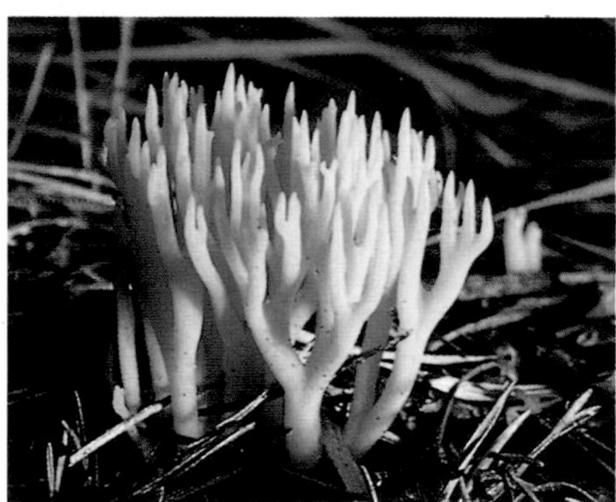

A common species recognized by the branched, orange-yellow, tough gelatinous fruitbodies which grow on conifer stumps.

Fruitbody ¾–3 in/2–8 cm high, bright orange-yellow, deeper orange when dry; erect, repeatedly branched, with a rooting base; surface smooth, rather slimy. *Flesh* tough, gelatinous, yellow. *Spore deposit* yellow. *Habitat* on old stumps of coniferous trees, especially pines. *Similar species* other species of *Calocera* are smaller, and have simple or sparsely branched fruitbodies. Species of *Clavaria* and allied genera differ in having brittle, non-gelatinous fruitbodies. All inedible. *Edibility* inedible.

GROUP Jelly Fungi
FAMILY Jelly Antler Fungus (Dacrymycetaceae)

SEASON  **EDIBILITY** 

HABITAT 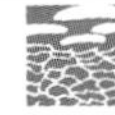 On trees, stumps or woody debris

GROUP Mushrooms and Toadstools
FAMILY Tricholoma (Tricholomataceae)

SEASON  **EDIBILITY** 

HABITAT  On the ground in grassland or open spaces

CALOCYBE GAMBOSA

St George's Mushroom

This large, whitish mushroom is usually much sought after as it is one of the few, good edible species to occur in spring.

Cap 2–4 in/5–10 cm in diameter, convex with a wavy, inrolled margin, white to pale brown, smooth and dry. *Gills* sinuate, white to cream, narrow and densely crowded. *Stem* $1\frac{1}{4}$–3 × $\frac{3}{8}$–1 in/3–8 × 1–2.5 cm, short and stocky, white, smooth, solid. *Flesh* thick, white, smelling of damp flour. *Spore deposit* white. *Habitat* among grass, preferring chalky soil. *Similar species* the spring appearance is likely to overcome confusion, but avoid collecting at the same time as the reddening *Inocybe* species and the white *Clitocybe* species, which grow in similar situations; poisonous. *Edibility* good.

GROUP Mushrooms and Toadstools
FAMILY Wax-gill (Hygrophoraceae)

SEASON  **EDIBILITY** 

HABITAT  On the ground in grassland or open spaces

CAMAROPHYLLUS PRATENSIS

Buff Meadow Cap *or* Salmon Wax Cap

A fleshy, orange-buff wax cap, which is regarded as a good, edible species.

Cap $1\frac{1}{4}$–$3\frac{1}{2}$ in/3–9 cm in diameter, convex, often with a raised centre, developing a wavy margin, orange-buff to tawny yellow, smooth, dry, sometimes cracking. *Gills* deeply decurrent, yellowish buff, thick and waxy, broadly spaced. *Stem* 2–3 × $\frac{3}{16}$–$\frac{3}{8}$ in/5–8 × 0.5–1 cm, cylindrical or tapering at the base, similarly coloured to cap but often paler, smooth. *Flesh* thick, white, firm. *Spore deposit* white. *Habitat* in open grassland, sometimes also found in frondose woodland. *Similar species C. colemannianus* is smaller, pinkish grey-brown and has a striated cap margin; edible. *Edibility* excellent.

CANTHARELLUS CIBARIUS

The Chanterelle *or* The Girolle

A bright orange-yellow, fleshy mushroom with thick branching ridges descending down the stem instead of thin gills.

Cap 1¼–6 in/3–15 cm in diameter, yellow to orange, convex then flattened, with a wavy, inrolled margin, dry surface. *Gills* decurrent, formed by thick folds and ridges. *Stem* short and tapering, 1¼–4 × 3⁄16–1 in/3–10 × 0.5–2.5 cm, solid, similarly coloured to cap. *Flesh* thick, pale yellow, with a mild smell of apricots. *Spore deposit* white. *Habitat* under beech and oak. *Similar species Hygrophoropsis aurantiaca,* page 37, which is inedible. *Edibility* excellent and much sought after.

GROUP Chanterelles
FAMILY Cantharellaceae

SEASON 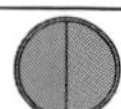 **EDIBILITY** 

HABITAT  On the ground in woodlands or associated with trees

CHLOROPHYLLUM MOLYBDITES

Green-Spored Lepiota

A large, white mushroom found on lawns which has green gills; a unique feature.

Cap 2–6 (–8) in/5–15 (–20) cm in diameter, ball-shaped soon expanding to broadly convex, covered by a dark brown layer which breaks up to expose a pure white background. *Gills* free, pale buff but later becoming deep green, staining reddish when bruised. *Stem* 4–8 × ⅝–1 in/10–20 × 1.5–2.5 cm, easily detached from the cap, cylindrical, whitish to pale greyish brown, fibrous, with a large, thick fleshy ring, becoming free and movable. *Flesh* pale pinkish, reddening on bruising, thick, with a pleasant odour. *Spore deposit* pea-green. *Habitat* among grass, including lawns; not present in Europe. *Similar species* frequently confused with the edible *Macrolepiota* species, which have white gills. Always take a spore print. *Edibility* **poisonous.**

GROUP Mushrooms and Toadstools
FAMILY Mushroom and Lepiota (Agaricaceae)

SEASON  **EDIBILITY** 

HABITAT  On the ground in grassland or open spaces

CLAVARIADELPHUS PISTILLARIS
Giant Club *or* Pestle-Shaped Coral

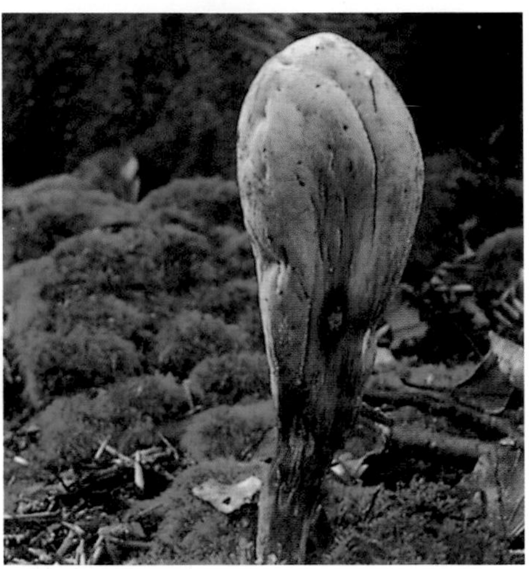

This is a large, club-shaped species. *Fruitbody* 4–9in/10–25cm tall and up to 6 cm in diameter, swollen club-shaped with a rounded apex tapering to a slender stem, ochre-yellow, progressively discolouring reddish brown towards the base, smooth or with a few vertical wrinkles. *Flesh* thick, firm, white bruising purplish brown. *Spore deposit* white. *Habitat* among leaf-litter in beech woods, or with pines at higher localities. *Similar species* unlikely to be confused with other species. *Edibility* edible after cooking.

GROUP Club Fungi
FAMILY Giant Club (Clavariadelphaceae)

SEASON  **EDIBILITY** 

HABITAT  On the ground in woodlands or associated with trees

CLAVULINA CRISTATA
Crested Coral Fungus

A very common coral fungus, with numerous, white branches.

Fruitbody ¾–2¾ in/2–7 cm in diameter, densely branched, white, with the individual branches terminating as crest-like tips; arising from an indistinct stalk-like base. *Flesh* white, soft. *Spore deposit* white. *Habitat* on the ground in deciduous and mixed woodland. *Similar species* the Grey Coral Fungus (*C. cinerea*) is very closely related but coloured ash-grey; edible. *Edibility* edible but poor.

GROUP Club Fungi
FAMILY Clavulina (Clavulinaceae)

SEASON 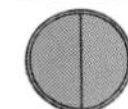 **EDIBILITY** 

HABITAT  On the ground in woodlands or associated with trees

CLAVULINOPSIS FUSIFORMIS

Golden Spindles

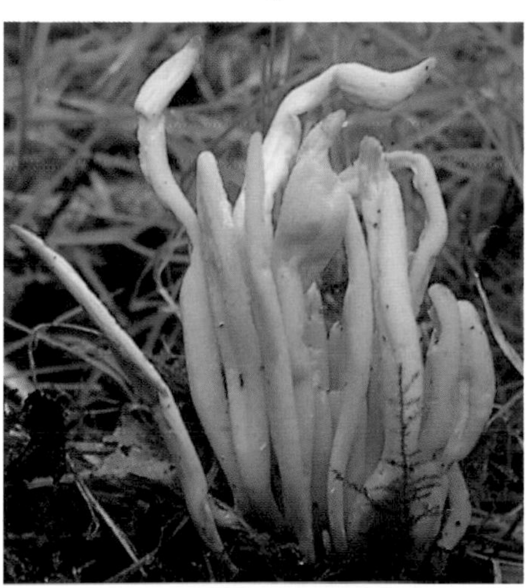

The fruitbody consists of tufts of bright yellow, slender clubs.

Fruitbody densely tufted, 2–5½ in/5–14 cm high, of bright yellow clubs which are fused at their base; individual clubs are 1⁄16–¼ in/0.2–0.6 cm wide, with a pointed tip. *Flesh* yellow, soft. *Spore deposit* white. *Habitat* among grass in field and woods. *Similar species C. luteoalba* is also yellow but has white, obtusely rounded tips; *C. helvola* has yellow but apically obtuse and non-tufted fruitbodies. Both species are inedible. *Edibility* inedible, with a bitter taste.

GROUP Club Fungi
FAMILY Fairy Club (Clavariaceae)

SEASON  **EDIBILITY** 

HABITAT  On the ground in grassland or open spaces

CLITOCYBE ODORA

Blue-Green Clitocybe *or* Anise-Scented Clitocybe

Distinguished by the bluish green cap, whitish gills, and smelling of anise.

Cap 1¼–2¾ in/3–7 cm in diameter, soon flattened or depressed, with an incurved, wavy margin, dingy bluish green, but sometimes blue or paling to almost white when dry, smooth. *Gills* slightly decurrent, whitish or tinged greenish, crowded. *Stem* 1¼–2¾ × 3⁄16–⅜ in/3–7 × 0.5–1 cm, whitish or greenish, with a woolly base. *Flesh* thin, pale, with a strong odour. *Spore deposit* white. *Habitat* prefers woodland, growing with oak; occasional. *Similar species C. fragrans* has a similar smell, but is slender, pale yellowish brown; inedible. *C. suaveolens* is also smaller, greyish white; inedible. *Edibility* edible, and can be dried for use as a condiment.

GROUP Mushrooms and Toadstools
FAMILY Tricholoma (Tricholomataceae)

SEASON  **EDIBILITY** 

HABITAT  On the ground in woodlands or associated with trees

CLITOPILUS PRUNULUS

The Miller *or* Sweetbread Mushroom

A whitish species, with decurrent gills, and a strong smell and taste of bread dough.

Cap 1¼–4 in/3–10 cm in diameter, convex to depressed with a wavy margin, white or with a greyish tint, dry and smooth. *Gills* deeply decurrent, white then pale pink, widely spaced. *Stem* 1¼–2 × ⅜–⅝ in/3–5 × 1–1.5 cm, short, sometimes excentric, white, smooth, solid. *Flesh* thick, white, with a very strong odour. *Spore deposit* salmon-pink. *Habitat* forms small groups on ground in open woodland and grassy glades. *Similar species* the poisonous *Clitocybe dealbata* grows in grassland, but has white, crowded gills, and lacks the mealy smell. *Edibility* excellent.

GROUP Mushrooms and Toadstools
FAMILY Entoloma (Entolomataceae)

SEASON 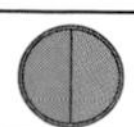 **EDIBILITY** 

HABITAT  On the ground in woodlands or associated with trees

COLLYBIA BUTYRACEA

Greasy Tough Shank

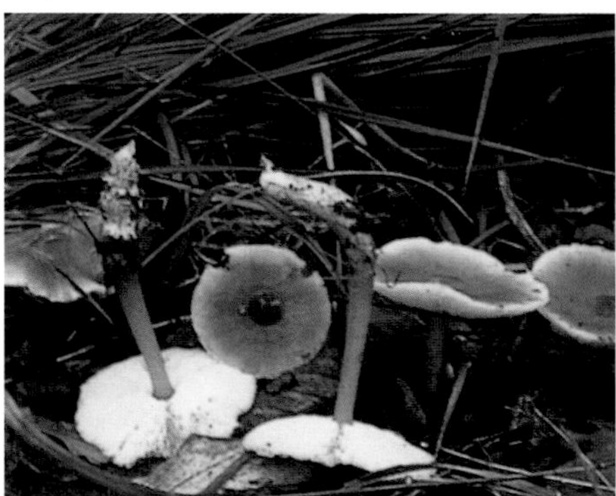

A common species, readily recognized by the brown cap with a greasy, raised centre, white gills, and a stem which is tough, fibrous and thicker towards the base.

Cap 1¼–3 in/3–8 cm in diameter, convex with a raised centre, yellowish brown to dark brown, drying paler but remaining dark at the centre, moist and greasy, smooth. *Gills* adnexed to free, whitish, crowded. *Stem* 1¼–2¼ × 3/16–⅜ in/3–6 × 0.5–1 cm, thicker downwards and often swollen at the base, of similar colour to the cap, becoming hollow. *Flesh* pale, fibrous, lacking a distinctive smell. *Spore deposit* white. *Habitat* in leaf-litter in both deciduous and coniferous woods. *Similar species* unlikely to be confused with other species. *Edibility* edible but poor and not recommended.

GROUP Mushrooms and Toadstools
FAMILY Tricholoma (Tricholomataceae)

SEASON  **EDIBILITY** 

HABITAT  On the ground in woodlands or associated with trees

COLLYBIA MACULATA
Spotted Tough Shank

A common species which can be readily recognized by the reddish brown spotting of the white cap, stem and gills.

Cap 1½–4 in/4–10 cm in diameter, convex becoming flattened and irregularly depressed, at first white soon becoming spotted with reddish brown, dry and smooth. *Gills* free to adnexed, whitish to pale cream, usually becoming spotted with reddish brown, narrow, very crowded. *Stem* 2–4 × 5⁄16–½ in/5–10 × 0.8–1.2 cm, tall, whitish but often spotted reddish brown, becoming hollow, tough, fibrous, and striated. *Flesh* white, firm, lacking a distinctive smell. *Spore deposit* cream to pale pinkish. *Habitat* often in troops in woodland. *Similar species* unlikely to be confused with other species. *Edibility* inedible owing to tough texture and a rather bitter taste.

GROUP Mushrooms and Toadstools
FAMILY Tricholoma (Tricholomataceae)

SEASON 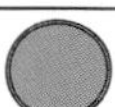 **EDIBILITY** 

HABITAT  On the ground in woodlands or associated with trees

COLTRICIA PERENNIS
Brown Funnel Polypore

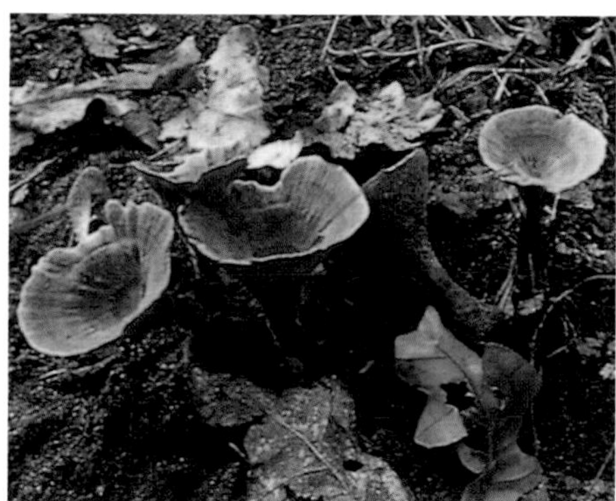

A polypore with a brown and zoned funnel-cap and slender, central stem.

Cap ¾–4 in/2–10 cm in diameter, circular with a depressed centre to almost funnel-shaped, golden brown to cinnamon-brown, finely velvety, with numerous concentric zones, and a thin, straight margin. *Tubes* decurrent, reddish brown; *pores* small, angular, rusty brown. *Stem* 1¼–2¾ × 3⁄16–⅜ in/3–7 × 0.5–1 cm, cylindrical, similarly coloured to the cap or darker, velvety, solid. *Flesh* firm, fibrous, brown. *Habitat* on sandy soil under conifers. *Similar species C. cinnamomea* is smaller, has a shiny cap, and grows in groups in deciduous woodland; inedible. *Edibility* inedible.

GROUP Bracket Fungi
FAMILY Brown Polypore (Hymenochaetaceae)

SEASON  **EDIBILITY** 

HABITAT  On the ground in woodlands or associated with trees

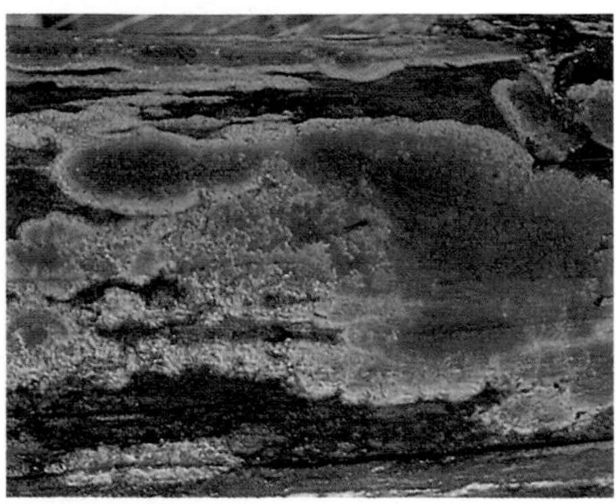

CONIOPHORA PUTEANA

Cellar Fungus *or* Wet Rot Fungus

A fungus commonly found in damp buildings on conifer wood, and distinguished by the olive-brown, warty surface and a whitish, cottony margin.

Fruitbody closely appressed to the woody substrate, up to 16 in/40 cm in diameter, and lacking a free margin, initially forming small, round patches about 1/16 in/0.1 cm thick; surface smooth to warty, cream to olive-brown or dark brown, with a whitish, finely fringed edge. *Flesh* membranous, fibrous. *Spore deposit* olive-brown. *Habitat* on dead wood, mainly of conifers; often found in damp buildings. *Similar species C. arida* has thinner fruitbodies; inedible. *Edibility* inedible.

GROUP Bracket fungi
FAMILY Dry and Wet Rot (Coniophoraceae)

SEASON 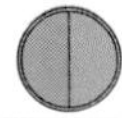 **EDIBILITY** 

HABITAT  On trees, stumps or woody debris

CONOCYBE TENERA

Brown Cone Cap

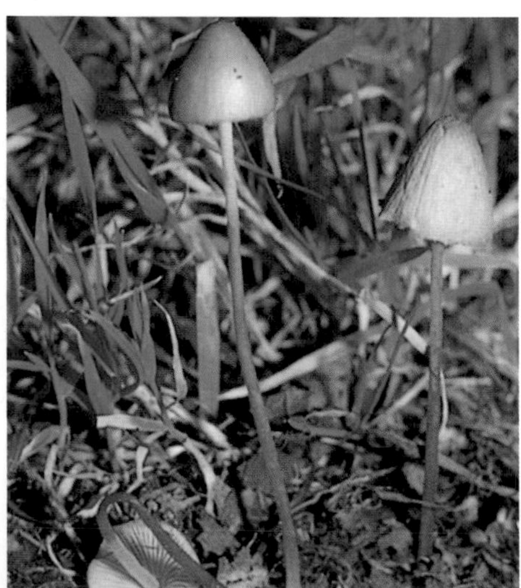

The conical, brown cap, brown gills, and grassland habitat identify this species.

Cap 3/8–1 1/4 in/1–3 cm in diameter, conical and remaining so, ochre-brown, sometimes paler, smooth and dry. *Gills* adnate, cinnamon-brown, narrow, fairly crowded. *Stem* 1 1/2–3 × 1/8 in/4–8 × 0.2–0.3 cm, slender, cylindrical, pale brown, darker towards the base. *Flesh* thin, cream-coloured. *Spore deposit* rusty brown. *Habitat* scattered, among grass or path edges in woodland. *Similar species* many cone caps are similar in appearance. *Edibility* inedible.

GROUP Mushrooms and Toadstools
FAMILY Bolbitius (Bolbitiaceae)

SEASON  **EDIBILITY** 

HABITAT  On the ground in grassland or open spaces

COPRINUS ATRAMENTARIUS
Common Ink-Cap *or* Alcohol Ink-Cap

A large ink-cap, forming tufts at the base of tree stumps.

Cap 2–2¾ in/5–7 cm in diameter, bell-shaped, grey, with a few tiny scales at centre, and finely grooved towards margin. *Gills* free, white becoming grey, finally dissolving into a black liquid. *Stem* 2¾–6 × ⅜–⅝ in/7–15 × 1–1.5 cm, cylindrical, white, hollow, faint ring at the base. *Flesh* thin, greyish, brittle. *Spore deposit* black. *Habitat* near tree-stumps. *Similar species C. acuminatus* is slender with pointed cap; *C. insignia* has warted spores. *Edibility* edible and good when young, must **never** be consumed with alcohol.

GROUP Mushrooms and Toadstools
FAMILY Ink-cap (Coprinaceae)

SEASON 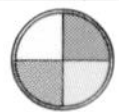 **EDIBILITY** 

HABITAT On the ground in grassland or open spaces

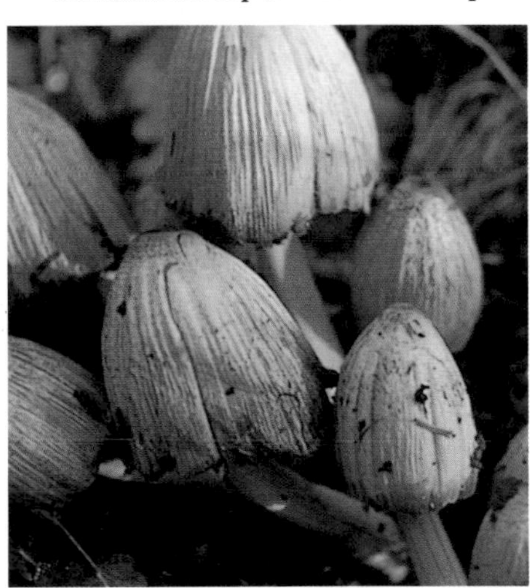

COPRINUS COMATUS
Shaggy Ink-Cap *or* Lawyer's Wig

A common, tufted species.

Cap tall, cylindrical, up to 5½ in/14 cm high, 1¼–2 in/3–5 cm across, with a rounded apex, white, covered with curled, woolly scales, dry, blackening from the margin upwards. *Gills* free, white becoming grey then black, dissolving to a black ink. *Stem* 2¼–8 × ⅜–¾ in/6–20 × 1–2 cm, cylindrical, white, hollow, movable ring. *Flesh* white, soft. *Spore deposit* black. *Habitat* grassland. *Similar species C. picaceus* grows in beechwoods; cap scales form white patches on black background; inedible. *Edibility* good when young.

GROUP Mushrooms and Toadstools
FAMILY Ink-cap (Coprinaceae)

SEASON 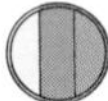 **EDIBILITY** 

HABITAT On the ground in grassland or open spaces

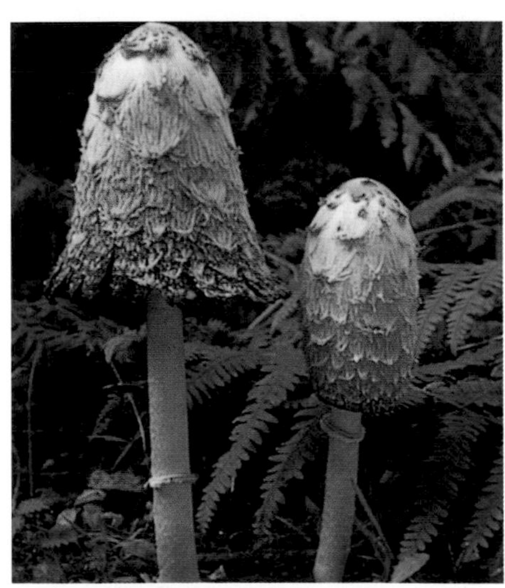

COPRINUS DISSEMINATUS

Trooping Crumble Caps *or* Non-Inky Coprinus

A tiny, bell-shaped ink-cap, growing in enormous numbers over the substratum.

Cap 3⁄16–3⁄8 in/0.5–1 cm in diameter, pale yellowish brown slowly becoming greyish, finely grooved, bearing minute hairs which are visible with a hand-lens. *Gills* adnate, at first white then progressively grey to black from the edge, broad, moderately spaced. *Stem* 3⁄8–1¼ × 1⁄16 in/1–3 × 0.1–0.2 cm, slender and brittle, fragile, hollow, white, smooth. *Flesh* thin and watery. *Spore deposit* dark brown. *Habitat* commonly found in great numbers over fallen, woodland debris, and can also be found in grassy areas. *Similar species* unlikely to be confused with other species. *Edibility* worthless.

GROUP Mushrooms and Toadstools
FAMILY Ink-cap (Coprinaceae)

SEASON 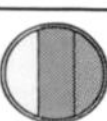 **EDIBILITY** 

HABITAT  On the ground in woodlands or associated with trees

CORDYCEPS MILITARIS

Trooping Cordyceps *or* Scarlet Caterpillar Fungus

A distinctive, club-shaped species recognized by the bright orange fruitbody with roughened head and smooth stem which arises from a buried, mummified caterpillar.

Fruitbody ¾–2¼ in/2–6 cm high, cylindrical-clavate, upper fertile part 3⁄16–¼ in/0.4–0.6 cm wide, bright orange or orange-red, cylindrical or irregular in shape, with a finely roughened surface. *Stem* 1⁄8–3⁄16 in/0.3–0.4 cm wide, cylindrical, flexuous, smooth, orange, slightly paler than the head. *Habitat* in grassland, arising singly or in clusters from buried, mummified larvae or pupae of butterflies or moths. *Similar species* unlikely to be confused with other species. *Edibility* inedible.

GROUP Flask Fungi
FAMILY Vegetable Caterpillar (Clavicipitaceae)

SEASON  **EDIBILITY** 

HABITAT  On the ground in grassland or open spaces

CORDYCEPS OPHIOGLOSSOIDES

Slender Truffle Cup *or* Golden-thread Cordyceps

Recognized by the blackish, ovoid fertile head, yellow stem and parasitic habit.

Fruitbody 2¼–4 in/6–10 cm high, club-shaped. *Fertile head* ⅝–1 × 5⁄16–1 × 5⁄16–½ in/1.5–2.5 × 0.8–1.3 cm, cylindrical or ovoid, at first yellow, smooth, becoming blackish and minutely roughened. *Stem* 1⁄16–⅛ in/0.2–0.3 cm wide, cylindrical, smooth, yellow. *Habitat* in woods, parasitic on *Elaphomyces* species. *Similar species C. canadensis* and *C. capitatus* occur on false truffles but have larger, capitate fruitbodies; both inedible. *Edibility* inedible.

GROUP Flask Fungi
FAMILY Vegetable Caterpillar (Clavicipitaceae)

SEASON  **EDIBILITY** 

HABITAT  On other fungi

CORIOLUS VERSICOLOR

Varicoloured Bracket *or* Turkey Tail

A common bracket-fungus, with thin, tough caps, a zoned surface and pale flesh.

Cap 1¼–3 in/3–8 cm in diameter, thin, fan-shaped, surface grey to reddish brown or black, with many narrow zones, at first velvety but becoming smooth on weathering. *Tubes* shallow, about 1⁄16 in/0.1–0.2 cm long, white; *pores* small, 3–5 per 1⁄16 in/0.1 cm, angular. *Flesh* white, tough. *Spore deposit* white. *Habitat* groups on dead deciduous trees and stumps. *Similar species C. hirsutus* is grey and hairy; usually on beech; *C. pubescens* is straw-coloured; both inedible. *Edibility* inedible.

GROUP Bracket Fungi
FAMILY Poroid Bracket (Coriolaceae)

SEASON  **EDIBILITY** 

HABITAT  On trees, stumps or woody debris

CORTINARIUS ARMILLATUS

Red-Banded Cortinarius *or* Bracelet Cortinarius

A large common species, with distinctive brick-red bands on the stems.

Cap 2–4 in/5–10 cm in diameter, fleshy, bell-shaped to flattened, moist, orange to tawny brown, smooth but streaky. *Gills* adnate, pale to dark rusty brown, broad and widely spaced. *Stem* 3–6 × ⅜–⅝ in/8–15 × 1–1.5 cm, tall, with an expanding base, solid, brown, with brick-red bands of veil on lower surface. *Flesh* whitish. *Spore deposit* cinnamon-brown. *Habitat* with birch, on heathland and woodland. *Similar species* unlikely to be confused. *Edibility* inedible.

GROUP Mushrooms and Toadstools
FAMILY Cortinarius (Cortinariaceae)

SEASON  **EDIBILITY** 

HABITAT  On the ground in woodlands or associated with trees

CRATERELLUS CORNUCOPIOIDES

Horn of Plenty *or* Black Trumpet

Dull-coloured, hollow, trumpet-shaped fruitbodies, with no ridges on the outer surface.

Cap ¾–3 in/2–8 cm in diameter, blackish brown, paler when dry, scaly, with a wavy margin, hollow in centre. *Outer surface* smooth, without gills, pale grey or darker, appearing powdery. *Stem* indistinct, short and hollow. *Flesh* thin, greyish, without distinctive smell. *Spore deposit* white. *Habitat* under beech or oak, forming large troops among fallen leaves. *Similar species* the North American *C. fallax,* also edible, differs in having a strong odour, and an ochraceous spore deposit. *Edibility* good, often used in stews.

GROUP Chanterelles
FAMILY Cantharellaceae

SEASON  **EDIBILITY** 

HABITAT  On the ground in woodlands or associated with trees

CREPIDOTUS MOLLIS
Soft Slipper Toadstool *or* Jelly Crepidotus

One of the larger slipper toadstools, recognized in the field by an elastic layer which is observed when the cap is pulled apart.

Cap 3/4–2 3/4 in/2–7 cm in diameter, kidney-shaped to shell-shaped, with a narrow, lateral attachment, pale yellowish brown, drying paler, with a striated margin. *Gills* radiating from a lateral attachment point, white becoming cinnamon-brown, crowded. *Stem* none. *Flesh* thin, white, with a gelatinized layer. *Spore deposit* snuff-brown. *Habitat* on dead and rotting branches, often in large numbers. *Similar species C. calolepsis* has small brown scales on the cap surface; inedible. *Edibility* inedible.

GROUP Mushrooms and Toadstools
FAMILY Crepidotus (Crepidotaceae)

SEASON 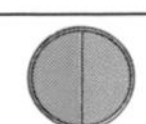 **EDIBILITY** 

HABITAT  On trees, stumps or woody debris

CYATHUS STRIATUS
Grooved Bird's Nest Fungus *or* Splash Cups

A distinctive species recognized by the brown, externally shaggy fruitbodies.

Fruitbody 1/4–5/8 in/0.7–1.5 cm high, 1/4–5/16 in/0.6–0.9 cm across, at first closed by a whitish membrane which ruptures and is soon lost at maturity; beaker-shaped, narrowed downwards; containing several egg-shaped fertile structures (peridioles). *Outer surface* reddish brown, densely covered with coarse, shaggy tufts of hairs. *Inner surface* pale, greyish or grey-brown, smooth, distinctly longitudinally grooved or furrowed. *Peridioles* ovoid, whitish or pale greyish, smooth, attached by a slender, whitish thread. *Habitat* in clusters, attached to twigs, leaves or other debris, often in gardens. *Similar species C. olla* has trumpet-shaped fruitbodies which are paler, felty on the surface; inedible. *Edibility* inedible.

GROUP Puffballs
FAMILY Bird's Nest Fungi (Nidulariaceae)

SEASON  **EDIBILITY** 

HABITAT  On trees, stumps or woody debris

CYSTODERMA AMIANTHINUM
Saffron Parasol *or* Pungent Cystoderma

A small, slender parasol mushroom, with a scaly, ochre-yellow cap and white gills.

Cap ¾–2 in/2–5 cm in diameter, conical to convex with a raised centre, dry, granular-scaly, with a shaggy margin. *Gills* adnate, white, narrow, crowded. *Stem* 1½–3 × ⅛ in/4–8 × 0.3–0.4 cm, tall and slender, hollow, granular-scaly below the ring, smooth above. *Ring* small, membranous, granular on the underside, pointing upwards. *Flesh* thin, pale, with an unpleasant mouldy smell. *Spore deposit* white. *Habitat* among conifer litter, and also found in mossy heathland. *Similar species* in North America, the variety *rugosoreticulatum* has a strongly wrinkled cap. Less common related species include *C. granulosum* which is darker reddish brown, and *C. carcharias* which is pinkish grey; all inedible. *Edibility* inedible.

GROUP Mushrooms and Toadstools
FAMILY Mushroom and Lepiota (Agaricaceae)

SEASON  **EDIBILITY** 

HABITAT  On the ground in woodlands or associated with trees

DAEDALEOPSIS CONFRAGOSA
Blood-Stained Bracket *or* Thin-Maze Flat Polypore

Commonly found bracket fungi, with a maze-patterned pore surface, which bruises pinkish brown.

Cap 2–6 in/5–15 cm in diameter, shelf-shaped with broad attachment, a convex to flattened upper surface, at first whitish then darkening to brown or purplish brown, with concentric zones and radial streaks. *Tubes* about ⅜ in/1 cm long, whitish to grey-brown; *pores* large, 1–2 per 1/16 in/0.1 cm, sometimes as round pores but often radially elongated or forming a maze pattern, white, bruising pinkish brown. *Flesh* about 3/16 in/0.5 cm thick, yellowish brown, tough and corky. *Spore deposit* white. *Habitat* on deciduous trees, especially alder, beech and willow. *Similar species* the variety *tricolor* is thinner, and blackish red with narrow zoning; inedible. *Edibility* inedible.

GROUP Bracket Fungi
FAMILY Poroid Bracket (Coriolaceae)

SEASON  **EDIBILITY** 

HABITAT  On trees, stumps or woody debris

DALDINIA CONCENTRICA

Cramp Balls *or* King Alfred's Cakes *or* Carbon Balls

A distinctive species having blackish, hemispherical fruitbodies of which the flesh has a distinctive concentric zonation.

Fruitbody ¾–3 in/2–8 cm across, subglobose or hemispherical, at first reddish brown, soon becoming black, shiny, smooth. *Flesh* rather fibrous, dark purplish brown or grey-brown, with conspicuous darker concentric zones. *Spore deposit* black. *Habitat* gregarious, on dead or dying deciduous trunks, especially ash and beech, also on charred birch; common. *Similar species D. vernicosa* has smaller fruitbodies which occur on burnt gorse; inedible. *Edibility* inedible.

GROUP Flask Fungi
FAMILY Candle Snuff (Xylariaceae)

SEASON 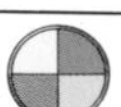 **EDIBILITY** 

HABITAT  On trees, stumps or woody debris

DERMOCYBE SANGUINEA

Blood-Red Cortinarius

A coniferous-wood species recognized by the blood-red cap, gills and stem.

Cap ¾–2 in/2–5 cm in diameter, dry, slightly felty, or scaly convex, becoming flattened, deep blood-red. *Gills* adnate, crowded, blood-red. *Stem* 2¼–3½ × ⅛–¼ in/6–9 × 0.3 0.6 cm, slender, cylindrical, slightly fibrillose, similarly coloured to the cap, with red cortina, slightly paler at the base. *Flesh* reddish, yielding a reddish juice when squashed, without any distinctive smell. *Spore deposit* rusty brown. *Habitat* in coniferous woods. *Similar species Cortinarius cinnabarinus* is similarly coloured but grows in beech woods; *C. anthracinus* occurs in pine woods but is brownish red and has a cap with a raised centre; *C. phoenicius* is also brownish red in colour and has brown flesh. All three species are poisonous. *Edibility* inedible.

GROUP Mushrooms and Toadstools
FAMILY Cortinarius (Cortinariaceae)

SEASON  **EDIBILITY** 

HABITAT  On the ground in woodlands or associated with trees

FISTULINA HEPATICA
Beefsteak Fungus

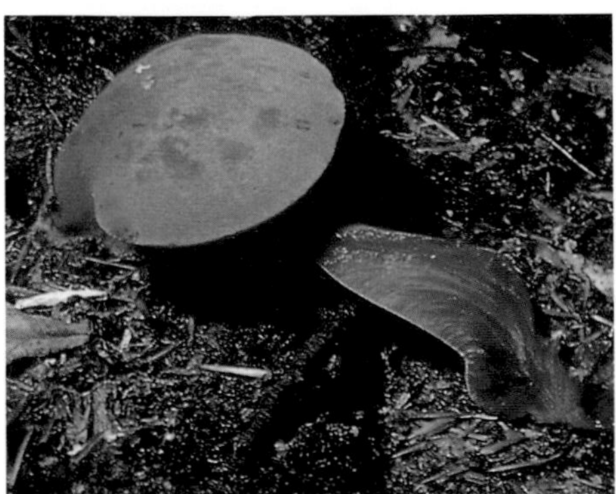

A large, reddish, fleshy bracket fungus, growing on oak trunks, and characterized by the tubes on the lower surface which are not fused to each other.

Cap 2¾–8 in/7–20 cm in diameter, tongue-like or bracket-shaped, convex and attached by a short, lateral stalk, pinkish to orange-red, with a sticky, roughened surface. *Tubes* up to ⅜ in/1 cm long, not fused but each developing separately; *pores* 2–3 per 1⁄16 in/0.1 cm, whitish or yellowish, bruising reddish brown. *Flesh* ¾–2 in/2–5 cm thick, succulent, whitish soon streaked with red. *Spore deposit* white to pale pink. *Habitat* on trunks of living or dead oak trees, sometimes chestnut. *Similar species* the individually separated tubes distinguish this from all other pore-fungi. *Edibility* edible but somewhat acidic.

GROUP Bracket Fungi
FAMILY Beefsteak Fungus (Fistulinaceae)

SEASON  **EDIBILITY** 

HABITAT 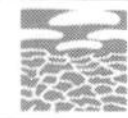 On trees, stumps or woody debris

FLAMMULINA VELUTIPES
Velvet Shank

A tufted mushroom, growing on trees during the winter months, recognized by the velvety stem and slimy cap.

Cap 1¼–2¼ in/3–6 cm in diameter, convex but soon flattened with a raised centre, reddish brown, sticky to slimy, smooth. *Gills* adnexed, white, broad, moderately spaced. *Stem* 1¼–2¾ × ⅛–3⁄16 in/3–7 × 0.3–0.5 cm, tough, tapering at the base, yellowish above becoming blackish brown below, finely velvety. *Flesh* soft, white. *Spore deposit* white. *Habitat* tufted on deciduous trees, especially elm. *Similar species* this species is grown commercially and sold under the name of "Eno-take"; however, the cultivated variety looks very different tending to be white, with a tiny cap, and very densely tufted. *Edibility* edible and collected throughout winter.

GROUP Mushrooms and Toadstools
FAMILY Tricholoma (Tricholomataceae)

SEASON  **EDIBILITY** 

HABITAT  On trees, stumps or woody debris

FOMES FOMENTARIUS

Tinder Fungus

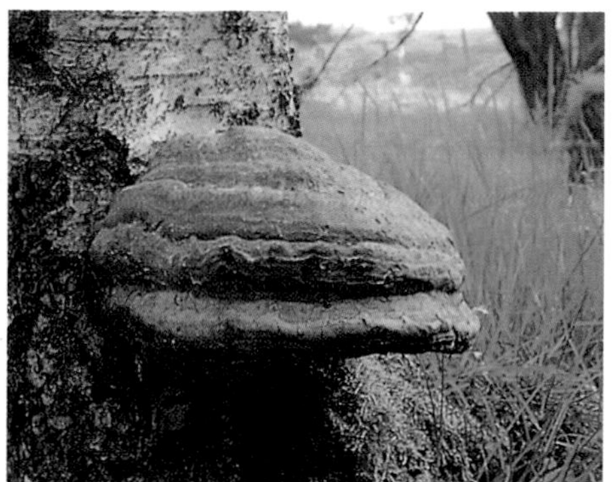

One of the largest of the bracket fungi, found on either beech or birch, forming hoof-shaped fruitbodies with a pale brown, corky flesh.

Cap 4–20 in/10–50 cm in diameter, very thick, horse hoof-shaped and layered, with a pale grey to blackish surface, smooth, and a broadly rounded margin. *Tubes* forming annual layers, each layer about ⅜ in/1 cm long; *pores* 3–4 per 1⁄16 in/0.1 cm, round, yellowish brown, bruising darker. *Flesh* up to 1¼ in/3 cm thick, pale brown, very tough and leathery. *Spore deposit* white. *Habitat* on birch, particularly in northern areas, and beech. *Similar species Phellinus igniarius* has a dark brown flesh, while *Fomitopsis pinicola* has a whitish pore surface, and the large *Ganoderma* species produce a brown spore deposit; all inedible. *Edibility* inedible.

GROUP Bracket Fungi
FAMILY Poroid Bracket (Coriolaceae)

SEASON 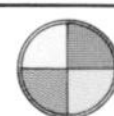 **EDIBILITY** 

HABITAT  On trees, stumps or woody debris

FOMITOPSIS PINICOLA

Red-Rimmed Bracket

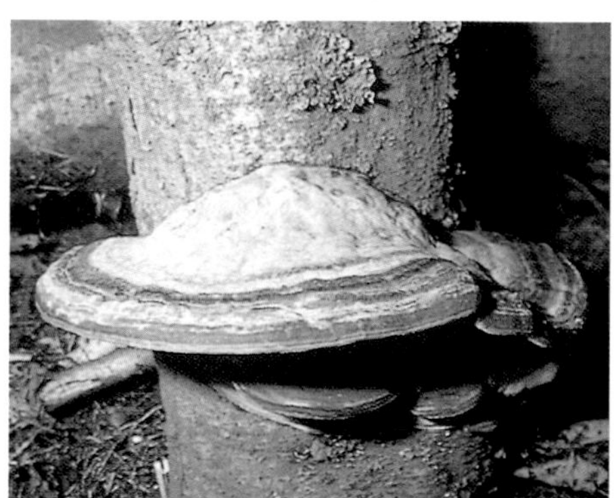

A common bracket fungus of spruce trees, distinguished by the resinous crust on the surface and the white flesh.

Cap 2–9 in/5–25 cm in diameter, very thick, hoof-shaped and layered with a thin, brittle, resinous crust, at first shiny yellow or reddish orange, finally black and dull, with a rounded, whitish margin. *Tubes* layered, each layer about ⅜ in/1 cm long; *pores* 3–4 per 1⁄16 in/0.1 cm, whitish, bruising grey. *Flesh* up to 1½ in/4 cm thick, whitish to cream-ochre, tough and corky. *Spore deposit* white. *Habitat* common, typically on spruce trees, but other hosts. *Similar species* the cream-coloured flesh distinguishes this from other *Phellinus* species. *Fomes fomentarius* (see this page) lacks the resinous crust. Both inedible. *Edibility* inedible.

GROUP Bracket Fungi
FAMILY Poroid Bracket (Coriolaceae)

SEASON 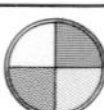 **EDIBILITY** 

HABITAT  On trees, stumps or woody debris

GANODERMA APPLANATUM

Artist's Fungus

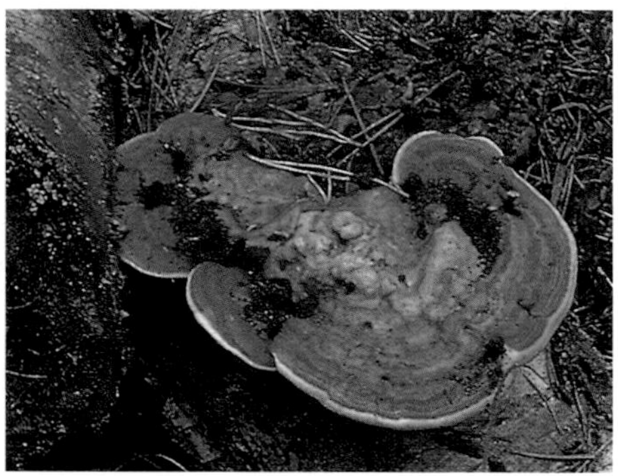

A large, perennial polypore recognized by the flat cap with a hard upper crust, and a white pore surface.

Cap 4–20 in/10–50 cm in diameter, plate-like, with the upper surface forming a dull, hard crust with indistinct concentric zones, at first pale brown then dark grey-brown (often covered with a spore deposit), and a thin, sharp margin. *Tubes* layered, each layer 3⁄16–3⁄8 in/0.5–1 cm long, brown; *pores* 5–6 per 1⁄16 in/0.1 cm, whitish becoming brownish. *Flesh* woody brown, often white flecks, corky, thinner than the tube-layer. *Spore deposit* cinnamon-brown. *Habitat* on dead wood, usually deciduous. *Similar species* often confused with *G. adspersum* where the dark brown flesh, lacks white flecks, is thicker than the tube-layer, and the round edge to the cap; inedible. *Edibility* inedible.

GROUP Bracket Fungi
FAMILY Ganoderma (Ganodermataceae)

SEASON 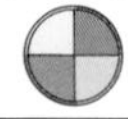 **EDIBILITY** 

HABITAT 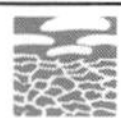 On trees, stumps or woody debris

GEASTRUM TRIPLEX

Collared Earthstar

One of the largest earthstars, with thick, star-like, fleshy rays, and a collar around the spore-sac.

Fruitbody up to 2¼ in/6 cm in diameter, in the young, unopened state resembling a tulip bulb. *Spore-sac* ¾–1½ in/2–4 cm in diameter, globose, greyish brown, containing a powdery spore-mass, with an apical pore surrounded by a fleshy collar. *Rays* 5–6, thick and fleshy, curved downwards, creamy brown, often cracked on the upper surface, greyish on the underside. *Spore deposit* dark brown at maturity. *Habitat* in groups among leaf-litter, under beech, preferring chalky soil. *Similar species G. pectinatum* is much thinner and smaller, with a short stalk, while the *G. saccatum* lacks both a stalk and a collar, both inedible. *Edibility* inedible.

GROUP Puffballs and allies
FAMILY Earthstar (Geastraceae)

SEASON 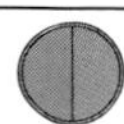 **EDIBILITY** 

HABITAT  On the ground in woodlands or associated with trees

GOMPHUS CLAVATUS

Pig's Ear Gomphus

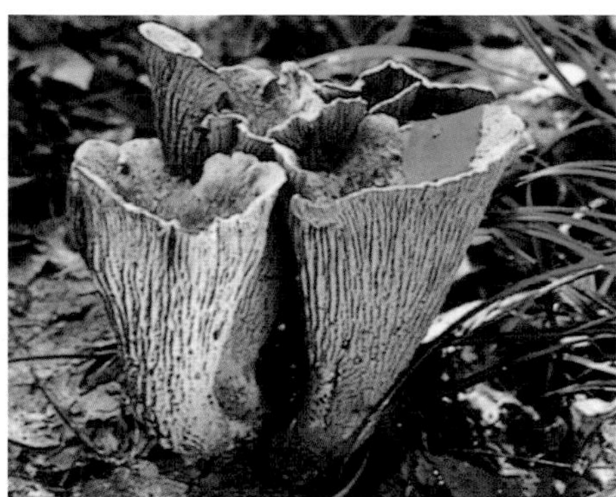

A thick, funnel-shaped, violaceous mushroom, having a strongly wrinkled to ridged undersurface, and growing in small clusters in coniferous forests.

Cap 1¼–4 in/3–10 cm in diameter, depressed with a raised wavy margin, smooth or slightly scaly, violet, eventually becoming yellowish brown. *Gills* strongly decurrent, reduced to narrow, indefinite, branching ridges, at first violet then fading. *Stem* ¾–2 × ⅜–¾ × 1–2 cm, short and thick, smooth, pale lilaceous brown. *Flesh* white and firm. *Spore deposit* ochre brown. *Habitat* small groups among leaf-litter; much more common in North America than in Europe where it is rare. *Similar species* the North American *C. floccosus* is a tall, hollow, reddish orange species, and is inedible. *Edibility* good.

GROUP Chanterelles
FAMILY Gomphaceae

SEASON  **EDIBILITY** 

HABITAT  On the ground in woodlands or associated with trees

GYMNOPILUS JUNONIUS

Orange Pholiota *or* Big Laughing Gymnopilus

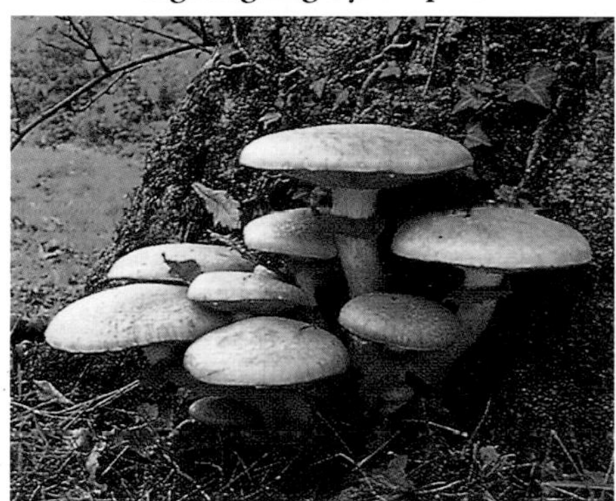

Often called *Pholiota spectabilis* in older books.

Cap 2¼–4¾ in/6–12 cm in diameter, convex, tawny brown to golden-brown, dry, radially streaky, surface breaking up into small scales. *Gills* adnate, yellowish to rusty brown, and crowded. *Stem* 2¼–6 × ⅜–1¼ in/6–15 × 1–3 cm, cylindrical, fibrous, similarly coloured or paler than the cap, with a large, brown, membranous ring near the apex. *Flesh* thick, yellowish. *Spore deposit* rusty brown. *Habitat* dense tufts at base of tree-trunks, especially ash and apple. *Similar species Pholiota squarrosa* has erect scales; the edible *Armillaria mellea* (page 13) has white, decurrent gills; while the poisonous *Omphalotus olearius* lacks a ring on the stem and produces white spores. *Edibility* **poisonous.**

GROUP Mushrooms and Toadstools
FAMILY Cortinarius (Cortinariaceae)

SEASON  **EDIBILITY** 

HABITAT  On trees, stumps or woody debris

GROUP Mushrooms and Toadstools
FAMILY Cortinarius (Cortinariaceae)

SEASON  **EDIBILITY** 

HABITAT  On trees, stumps or woody debris

GYMNOPILUS PENETRANS

Freckle-Gilled Gymnopilus

A very common toadstool, found in large numbers in conifer woods in the autumn, with a tawny brown cap and rusty brown, spotted gills.

Cap 1¼–2¼ in/3–6 cm in diameter, bell-shaped then flattened with a raised centre, tawny yellow, at times fading, smooth, dry, radially streaky. *Gills* 1¼–2¼ × ⅛–¼ in/3–6 × 0.3–0.7 cm, cylindrical, yellowish brown but with a whitish base. *Flesh* thin, yellowish. *Spore deposit* rusty brown. *Habitat* very common in coniferous woods, growing on fallen debris. *Similar species G. sapineus* has a more scaly cap, while *G. hybridus* has a cobweb-like veil; both inedible. *Edibility* inedible, with a bitter taste.

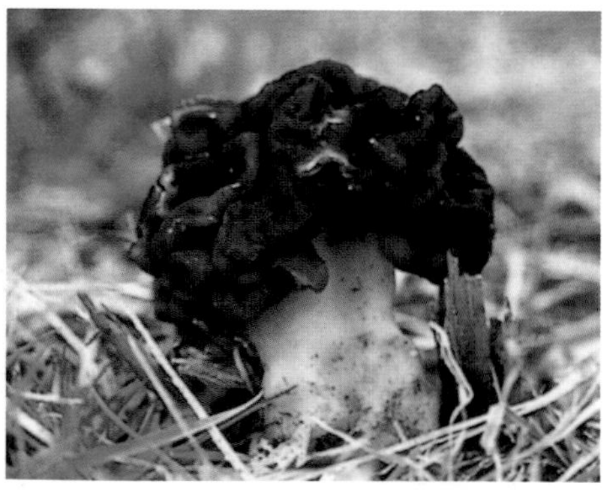

GROUP Cup Fungi
FAMILY Saddle-cup (Helvellaceae)

SEASON  **EDIBILITY** 

HABITAT  On the ground in woodlands or associated with trees

GYROMITRA ESCULENTA

Turban Fungus *or* False Morel

A conifer-wood species having a much-lobed, brain-like, reddish brown cap.

Cap 1¼–3½ in/3–9 cm across, much lobed and convoluted, brain-like in appearance, reddish brown. *Stem* ¾–2 × ¾–1½ in/2–5 × 2–4 cm, whitish or pale flesh coloured, often irregularly grooved, smooth or slightly scurfy. *Flesh* lacking a distinctive smell, whitish, thin, brittle, fruitbody internally chambered and hollow. *Habitat* with conifers, especially pines, growing on sandy soil. *Similar species* there are several other species of *Gyromitra*, especially in America. These may differ in shape and colour, but require microscopic examination for positive identification. *Edibility* **poisonous; deadly if eaten raw and sometimes harmful even after cooking.**

HEBELOMA CRUSTULINIFORME

Fairy Cake Hebeloma *or* Poison Pie

GROUP Mushrooms and Toadstools
FAMILY Cortinarius (Cortinariaceae)

SEASON  **EDIBILITY** 

HABITAT  On the ground in woodlands or associated with trees

A common, clay-brown species which has a strong smell of radish and exudes droplets from the gills in damp weather.

Cap 1½–3 in/4–8 cm in diameter, convex then expanding, with the margin remaining inrolled, buff to clay-brown, paler towards the margin, moist, smooth. *Gills* sinuate, pale clay-brown, crowded, exuding watery droplets in damp weather, dark brown spotted when dry. *Stem* 1½–2¾ × ⅜–¾ in/4–7 × 1–2 cm, cylindrical, thickened at the base, whitish, powdery especially towards the apex. *Flesh* thick, whitish, with a smell of radish. *Spore deposit* rusty brown. *Habitat* in deciduous woodland. *Similar species H. longicaudum* is larger, with a long stem and lacks the radish smell; poisonous. *Edibility* **poisonous**, with a bitter taste.

HELVELLA CRISPA

Common White Helvella *or* Fluted White Helvella

A common species with a whitish, saddle-shaped cap and furrowed stalk.

Cap ¾–2 in/2–5 cm across, saddle-shaped, lobed, convoluted at the centre, lobes not attached to the stalk, fertile upper surface whitish, smooth, lower surface pale buff, minutely downy. *Stem* ¾–3 × ⅜–1 in/2–8 × 1–2.5 cm, whitish with vertical grooves, hollow. *Flesh* thin, brittle, white. *Habitat* in woodland, often at path edges. *Similar species H. lacunosa* is similar in form, but has a dark grey or blackish cap and stem; inedible. *Edibility* edible but worthless.

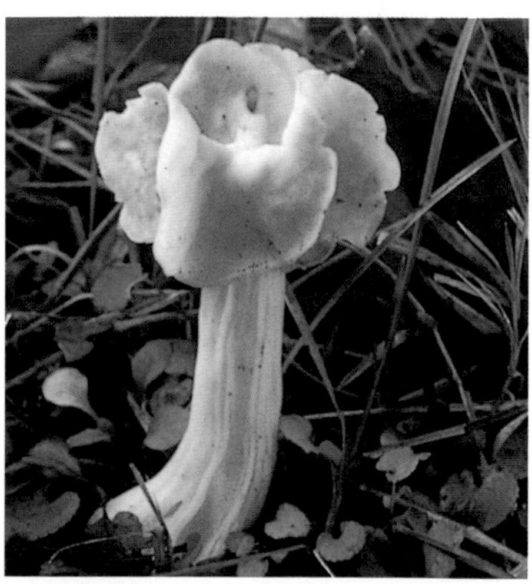

GROUP Cup Fungi
FAMILY Saddle-cup (Helvellaceae)

SEASON 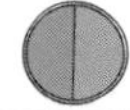 **EDIBILITY** 

HABITAT  On the ground in woodlands or associated with trees

HYGROCYBE CONICA

Conical Wax Cap *or* Witch's Hat

The most common of the brightly coloured wax caps which blacken at maturity.

Cap ¾–2 in/2–5 cm in diameter, conical and pointed, bright orange but progressively blackening with age, finely streaky, shiny, sticky. *Gills* adnexed, at first white later becoming greyish orange, and finally black, broad, widely spaced. *Stem* 2–4 × 3⁄16–⅜ in/5–10 × 0.5–1 cm, cylindrical, fibrous and splitting easily, yellowish. *Flesh* thin, watery, pale. *Spore deposit* white. *Habitat* commonly found anywhere among grass. *Similar species H. nigrescens* is more robust; poisonous. *H. conicoides* has a more rounded cap; inedible. *Edibility* inedible, to be avoided.

GROUP Mushrooms and Toadstools
FAMILY Wax-gill (Hygrophoraceae)

SEASON 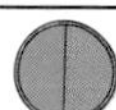 **EDIBILITY** 

HABITAT  On the ground in grassland or open spaces

HYGROCYBE PSITTACINA

Parrot Toadstool

A fairly common wax cap which may be difficult to recognize as it changes in colour and loses all greenish tints with age.

Cap ¾–2 in/2–5 cm in diameter, conical or bell-shaped, at first covered with a dark greenish slime, often with ochre, tawny red or pinkish tints. *Gills* adnate to short decurrent, greenish to yellowish, waxy, more or less spaced. *Stem* ¾–2 × 1⁄16–⅜ in/2–5 × 0.2–1 cm, cylindrical, greenish then developing yellow to orange or pink tints, slimy. *Flesh* thin, watery, pale. *Spore deposit* white. *Habitat* in coniferous or mixed woods, or grassland. *Similar species H. citrinovirens* has a sulphur-yellow cap which acquires green tints; edibility unknown. *Edibility* edible.

GROUP Mushrooms and Toadstools
FAMILY Wax-gill (Hygrophoraceae)

SEASON 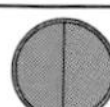 **EDIBILITY** 

HABITAT  On the ground in grassland or open spaces

HYGROPHOROPSIS AURANTIACA
False Chanterelle

A distinctive, pine-wood toadstool recognized by the orange colours and thin, crowded, much-forked, decurrent gills.

Cap 1–3 in/2.5–8 cm in diameter, convex at first, later depressed, incurved at the margin, orange-yellow (whitish in variety *pallida*), soft, dry, slightly felty. *Gills* decurrent, deep orange (cream in variety *pallida*), thin, crowded, much forked. *Stem* 1–2¾ × 3⁄16–⅜ in/2.5–7 × 0.4–1 cm, cylindrical or tapered, yellowish or orange-brown, often curved. *Flesh* yellowish (whitish in variety *pallida*). *Spore deposit* white. *Habitat* in pine woods and on heaths, often in troops. *Similar species* often confused with *Cantharellus cibarius,* page 17, but has thin gills and is orange rather than ochre-yellow; edible. *Edibility* inedible.

GROUP Boletes
FAMILY Paxillus (Paxillaceae)

SEASON  **EDIBILITY** 

HABITAT  On the ground in woodlands or associated with trees

HYPHOLOMA FASCICULARE
Sulphur Tuft

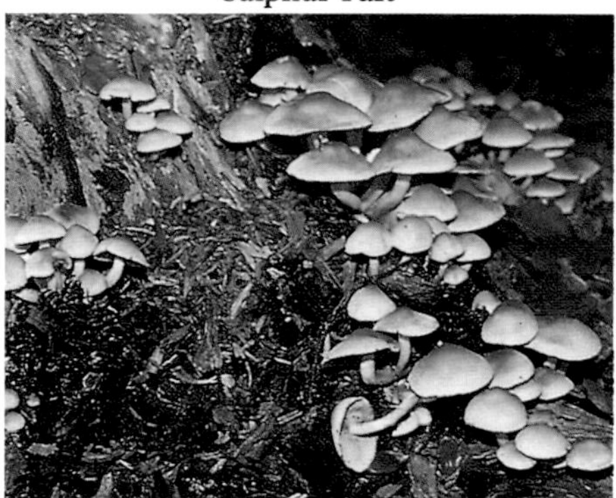

A common species recognized by the yellow cap and stem, greenish gills and densely clustered habit.

Cap ¾–2 in/2–5 cm across, convex, becoming flattened around a raised centre; pale sulphur-yellow, usually more red-brown at the centre; smooth, bearing remnants of the veil at the margin. *Gills* sulphur-yellow when young, becoming olive-green, sinuate, crowded. *Stem* 1½–3 × 3⁄16–5⁄16 in/4–8 × 0.5–0.9 cm, often curved, similarly coloured to the cap, smooth or bearing fibrils. *Flesh* thin, yellow. *Spore deposit* purple-brown. *Habitat* dense clusters on and around old stumps and logs of deciduous trees; common. *Similar species H. sublateritium* has a brick-red cap and lacks olive-green gills. *H. capnoides* also lacks green gills, and occurs on coniferous stumps; edible. *Edibility* inedible.

GROUP Mushrooms and Toadstools
FAMILY Stropharia (Strophariaceae)

SEASON 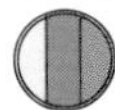 **EDIBILITY** 

HABITAT  On trees, stumps or woody debris

GROUP Mushrooms and Toadstools
FAMILY Cortinarius (Cortinariaceae)

SEASON  EDIBILITY 

HABITAT  On the ground in woodlands or associated with trees

INOCYBE FASTIGIATA

Peaked Inocybe *or* Straw-Coloured Fibre Head

A very common, species, with a yellowish brown cap; smells of mouldy bread.

Cap 2–2¾ in/5–7 cm in diameter, strongly conical, often splitting at the margin, straw-yellow to yellowish ochre, with radial fibrils which separate to reveal a paler background. *Gills* adnate, clay-brown, often with an olive tint, narrow, crowded. *Stem* 1½–4 × 3⁄16–5⁄16 in/4–10 × 0.5–0.8 cm, tall, cylindrical, white to ochre-brown, fibrous, hollow. *Flesh* pale, firm, with a distinctive smell. *Spore deposit* pale clay-brown. *Habitat* under trees, often beech. *Similar species I. maculata* has darker, reddish brown fibres on the cap; inedible. *Edibility* **poisonous, must be avoided.**

GROUP Mushrooms and Toadstools
FAMILY Cortinarius (Cortinariaceae)

SEASON 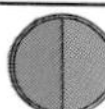 EDIBILITY 

HABITAT  On the ground in woodlands or associated with trees

INOCYBE GEOPHYLLA

Common White Inocybe *or* White Fibre Head

A small, shining, white toadstool, with brown gills, and an earthy smell.

Cap ⅜–1¼ in/1–3 cm in diameter, conical with raised centre and incurved margin, silky white with pale ochraceous centre, radially fibrous. *Gills* adnexed, ochraceous to clay-brown, crowded. *Stem* 1¼–2 × ⅛ in/3–5 × 0.3–0.4 cm, cylindrical, silky white. *Flesh* white, thin but firm, with earthy smell. *Spore deposit* clay-brown. *Habitat* in troops in woodland; very common. *Similar species I. geophylla* var. *lilacina* is identical except for the lilac colour; poisonous. *Edibility* **poisonous.**

KUEHNEROMYCES MUTABILIS

Two-tone Pholiota *or* Changing Pholiota

A clustered toadstool with a brown, two-toned cap and ringed brown stem.

Cap 1¼–2¼ in/3–6 cm across, convex, expanding, orange- or date-brown, soon drying pale ochraceous, smooth. *Gills* pale brown, slightly decurrent, crowded. *Stem* 1¼–3 × 3⁄16–⅜ in/3–8 × 0.5–1 cm, pale yellowish, smooth above a thin, brown ring, dark brown and scaly below. *Flesh* whitish or pale yellow. *Spore deposit* deep ochre. *Habitat* on deciduous trees. *Similar species* the deadly poisonous *Galerina unicolor* has a brownish cap and lacks the scaly stem. *Edibility* edible, but take care to avoid confusion.

GROUP Mushrooms and Toadstools
FAMILY Stropharia (Strophariaceae)

SEASON  **EDIBILITY** 

HABITAT 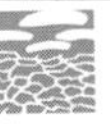 On trees, stumps or woody debris

LACCARIA AMETHYSTEA

Amethyst Deceiver

A very common, deep violet-coloured species growing in troops in woodland.

Cap ¾–2¼ in/2–6 cm in diameter, convex then flattened, with wavy margin, slightly scurfy, deep purplish violet, powdery near the top, and with a downy, lilac coating at the base. *Gills* violet, thick, widely spaced, adnate or slightly decurrent. *Stem* 1¼–3 × 3⁄16–¼ in/3–8 × 0.4–0.6 cm, fibrous, tough, similarly coloured to the cap. *Flesh* thin, fibrous, pale lilac, often becoming hollow in the stem; smell not distinctive. *Spore deposit* white. *Habitat* in deciduous and coniferous woods, usually in troops. *Similar species* the Deceiver *(L. laccata)* is of similar size and form. It differs in colour but similarly fades with age is also edible but tasteless. *Edibility* edible.

GROUP Mushrooms and Toadstools
FAMILY Tricholoma (Tricholomataceae)

SEASON  **EDIBILITY** 

HABITAT  On the ground in woodlands or associated with trees

LACCARIA LACCATA
The Deceiver

One of the most common species but very variable in appearance, recognized by the pinkish brown fruitbodies with widely spaced, "powdery" gills.

Cap 3/8–1½ in/1–4 cm in diameter, convex, soon becoming flattened or depressed, wavy at the margin, pinkish brown when moist, drying pale ochre or whitish, scurfy. *Gills* adnexed to slightly decurrent, pinkish brown. *Stem* 1¼–3 × 3/16–¼ in/3–8 × 0.4–0.6 cm, tall and twisted, fibrous-tough, similarly coloured to the cap. *Flesh* thin, pale, odourless. *Spore deposit* white. *Habitat* in scattered troops, among leaf-litter in woods. *Similar species L. proxima* is more robust and often found in damper situations; edible. *L. trullisata* is commonly found growing in sand in North America; edible. *Edibility* edible but tasteless.

GROUP Mushrooms and Toadstools
FAMILY Tricholoma (Tricholomataceae)

SEASON  **EDIBILITY** 

HABITAT  On the ground in woodlands or associated with trees

LACTARIUS DELICIOSUS
Saffron Milk-Cap

A large species, commonly found in pine woods, forming large troops; and distinguished by the orange colours.

Cap 2–8 in/5–20 cm in diameter, convex, soon depressed with an incurved margin, reddish orange with several darker zones, slimy when moist, staining green. *Gills* adnate to short decurrent, pale orange-yellow, staining green, crowded. *Stem* 1¼–3 × 3/8–5/8 in/3–8 × 1–1.5 cm, short, orange, often pitted, staining greenish. *Flesh* thick, yellowish cream, with an orange latex, and a fruity odour. *Spore deposit* pale pinkish cream. *Habitat* often in large numbers under conifers, especially pines. *Similar species L. deterrimus* has paler gills, and the stem is not pitted; edible. *Edibility* moderately good, with a mild taste.

GROUP Mushrooms and Toadstools
FAMILY Brittle-gills and Milk-caps (Russulaceae)

SEASON  **EDIBILITY** 

HABITAT  On the ground in woodlands or associated with trees

LACTARIUS RUFUS
Rufous Milk-Cap *or* Red-Hot Milk-Cap

A commonly found species of coniferous woodland, distinguished by the umbonate, reddish brown cap, and very peppery milk.

Cap 1½–4 in/4–10 cm in diameter, convex to flat or depressed with a raised centre, dull bay red, dry, with an incurved margin. *Gills* short decurrent, white to buffy brown, crowded. *Stem* 2–3 × 3⁄16–3⁄8 in/5–8 × 0.5–1 cm, dingy purplish brown, with a white base. *Flesh* fairly thin, pale purplish, with abundant, unchanging white latex. *Spore deposit* pinkish buff. *Habitat* on soil under pines, or in *Sphagnum* bogs. *Similar species L. hepaticus* is smaller, has a liver-brown cap, and a latex which discolours yellowish; inedible. *Edibility* not eaten in Western countries, owing to the acrid taste, yet sold commercially in Finland.

GROUP Mushrooms and Toadstools
FAMILY Brittle-gills and Milk-caps (Russulaceae)

SEASON 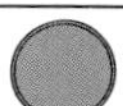 **EDIBILITY** 

HABITAT  On the ground in woodlands or associated with trees

LACTARIUS TORMINOSUS
Woolly Milk-Cap *or* Pink-Fringed Milk-Cap

The shaggy, zoned cap with a strongly inrolled margin distinguishes this birchwood species.

Cap 2–6 in/5–15 cm in diameter, convex to strongly depressed, pale salmon-pink, with several concentric zones, sticky when wet, with a shaggy, incurved margin. *Gills* adnate to decurrent, pale pinkish, crowded. *Stem* 1¼–3 × 3⁄16–5⁄8 in/3–8 × 0.5–1.5 cm, smooth, dry, pinkish but paler than the cap. *Flesh* white to pink, with a white, unchanging latex. *Spore deposit* pale pinkish cream. *Habitat* always with birch, in damp situations. *Similar species L. pubescens* has a whitish cap, while *L. mairei* is orange-coloured; both poisonous. *Edibility* **poisonous.**

GROUP Mushrooms and Toadstools
FAMILY Brittle-gills and Milk-caps (Russulaceae)

SEASON  **EDIBILITY** 

HABITAT  On the ground in woodlands or associated with trees

LAETIPORUS SULPHUREUS

Sulphur Polypore *or* Chicken of the Woods

The fruitbody forms large clusters of overlapping, sulphur-yellow caps, growing on the trunks of both living and dead trees.

Cap 2–8 in/5–20 cm in diameter, fan-shaped, flattened but up to 2 in/5 cm thick, with an orange, lemon-yellow or sulphur-yellow surface becoming paler when old except for the margin, smooth. *Tubes* forming a narrow layer, about 3⁄16 in/0.4 cm deep; *pores* small, 3–5 per 1⁄16 in/0.1 cm, round, sulphur-yellow. *Flesh* thick, pale yellowish cream to almost white, at first soft and moist but becoming crumbly like chalk. *Spore deposit* white. *Habitat* clustered on living trees, generally preferring oak and yew. *Similar species* the distinctive yellow brackets distinguish this species from other polypores. *Edibility* edible.

GROUP Bracket Fungi
FAMILY Poroid Bracket (Coriolaceae)

SEASON 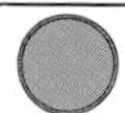 **EDIBILITY** 

HABITAT  On trees, stumps or woody debris

LANGERMANNIA GIGANTEA

Giant Puffball

Probably the easiest fungi to recognize, forming large ball-shaped structures.

Fruitbody 6–24 (–63) in/15–60 (–160) cm in diameter, ball-shaped or nearly so, rather flattened in large specimens, at first pure white, with a smooth, soft surface and a texture of suede, later discolouring yellowish to olive-brown with the outer layer gradually flaking away. *Flesh* white and firm but progressively becoming brown and powdery as the spores mature. *Spore deposit* brown. *Habitat* singly or in groups, sometimes forming large fairy rings, in field and on road verges. *Similar species* No species grows to this size; *Calvatia excipuliformis* forms fruitbodies up to 4 in/10 cm in diameter, but has a basal stalk; edible. *Edibility* edible and delicious when young and the flesh is white and firm.

GROUP Puffballs and Allies
FAMILY Puffball (Lycoperdaceae)

SEASON  **EDIBILITY** 

HABITAT  On the ground in grassland or open spaces

LECCINUM SCABRUM

Brown Birch Bolete *or* Common Scabre Stalk

A very common species, belonging to a group sometimes known as the "rough shanks". This species has a greyish brown cap and blackish stem scales.

Cap 1½–4 in/4–10 cm in diameter, strongly convex, thick fleshed, greyish brown to yellowish brown, smooth, dry to sticky. *Tubes* adnexed, deeply sunken around the stem apex, off-white; *pores* off-white, minute, bruising brownish. *Stem* 2¾–6 × ¾–1¼ in/ 7–15 × 2–3 cm, tall, off-white, with tiny, black, granular scales. *Flesh* thick, soft, white, unchanging or with slight pink-brown flush. *Spore deposit* cinnamon-brown. *Habitat* on the ground, under birch trees. *Similar species L. holopus* has a white cap and grows with birch, while *L. vulpinus* is purplish brown and grows with pine; both edible. *Edibility* edible and excellent.

GROUP Boletes
FAMILY Boletus (Boletaceae)

SEASON 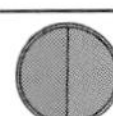 **EDIBILITY** 

HABITAT  On the ground in woodlands or associated with trees

LENTINUS LEPIDEUS

Scaly Lentinus

A tough, whitish toadstool which forms groups on decayed conifer wood.

Cap 1¼–6 in/3–15 cm in diameter, firm, convex to depressed, white to pale yellow, dry, smooth or breaking up into fibrous scales in concentric rings; margin at first inrolled. *Gills* shortly decurrent, whitish, broad, moderately crowded, with a toothed edge. *Stem* ¾–4¼ × ⅜–¾ in/2–11 × 1–2 cm, central or nearly so, cylindrical, solid, similarly coloured to cap with indistinct scales, and a poorly developed ring near the gill attachment. *Flesh* about ⅜ in/1 cm thick, white, firm. *Spore deposit* white. *Habitat* solitary or in small groups on dead trunks and roots of conifers. *Similar species L. ponderosus* of North America, is more fleshy and lacks a ring on the stem; inedible. *Edibility* edible, but not recommended.

GROUP Mushrooms and Toadstools
FAMILY Lentinus and Oyster Cap (Lentinaceae)

SEASON  **EDIBILITY** 

HABITAT  On trees, stumps or woody debris

LEOTIA LUBRICA

Jelly Babies *or* Ochre Jelly Club

A distinctive species recognized by the gelatinous fruitbody with yellowish stalk and olive-yellow head.

Fruitbody 3⁄4–2 1⁄4 in/2–6 cm high, capitate, gelatinous. *Fertile head* 3⁄16–3⁄8 in/0.4–1 cm across, convex, irregularly lobed at the margin, yellowish green or olivaceous, smooth, rather slimy. *Stalk* 1⁄8–5⁄16 in/0.3–0.8 cm wide, cylindrical, tapered at the base, ochraceous, covered in tiny, greenish granules. *Flesh* yellowish, gelatinous, becoming hollow in the stem, without a distinctive smell. *Spore deposit* white. *Habitat* on damp ground in deciduous woodland, gregarious or clustered. *Similar species L. atrovirens,* in North America, differs in being wholly green, and *L. viscosa,* also in North America, has a dark green head; both inedible. *Edibility* inedible.

GROUP Cup Fungi
FAMILY Jelly Discs (Leotiaceae)

SEASON 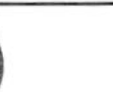 **EDIBILITY** 

HABITAT  In wet situations, such as bogs and marshlands

LEPIOTA CRISTATA

Stinking Parasol *and* Malodorous Lepiota

The small white caps have concentric rings of reddish brown scales, the gills are white, and there is a ring on the stem.

Cap 3⁄4–1 1⁄2 in/2–4 cm in diameter, convex to almost flat, often with a raised centre, white except for the dark centre and rings of small scales. *Gills* free, narrow, and very crowded. *Stem* 3⁄4–2 3⁄4 × 1⁄8–3⁄16 in/2–7 × 0.2–0.5 cm, slender, hollow, white and smooth, with a small, fragile ring attached to the upper region. *Flesh* thin, white, with an unpleasant, rubbery smell. *Spore deposit* white. *Habitat* grows in small troops among leaf-litter or short grass, often at the edge of woods. *Similar species L. clypeolaria* is larger, with pale yellowish brown scales on both cap and stem, while *L. castanea* has chestnut-brown scales, and a different smell; both poisonous. *Edibility* possibly **poisonous.**

GROUP Mushrooms and Toadstools
FAMILY Mushroom and Lepiota (Agaricaceae)

SEASON  **EDIBILITY** 

HABITAT  On the ground in woodlands or associated with trees

LEPISTA INVERSA
Tawny Funnel Cap

Recognized by the wavy, reddish brown cap and crowded, pale yellowish gills. Formerly called *Clitocybe flaccida*.

Cap 1½–4 in/4–10 cm in diameter, soon depressed, becoming much paler on drying. *Gills* decurrent, thin, very crowded. *Stem* 1¼–2¼ × 3⁄16–⅜ in/3–6 × 0.5–1 cm, paler than cap, becoming hollow and often flattened, smooth with a hairy base. *Flesh* thin, whitish, with an earthy smell. *Spore deposit* pale pinkish cream. *Habitat* clustered among fallen leaves, sometimes forming fairy rings. *Similar species L. gilva* is restricted to coniferous woodland, and has a pale yellow cap; it is edible. *Edibility* caps good but slightly acidic to some tastes; stems too tough.

GROUP Mushrooms and Toadstools
FAMILY Tricholoma (Tricholomataceae)

 **SEASON**  **EDIBILITY** 

HABITAT  On the ground in woodlands or associated with trees

LEPISTA NUDA
Wood Blewit

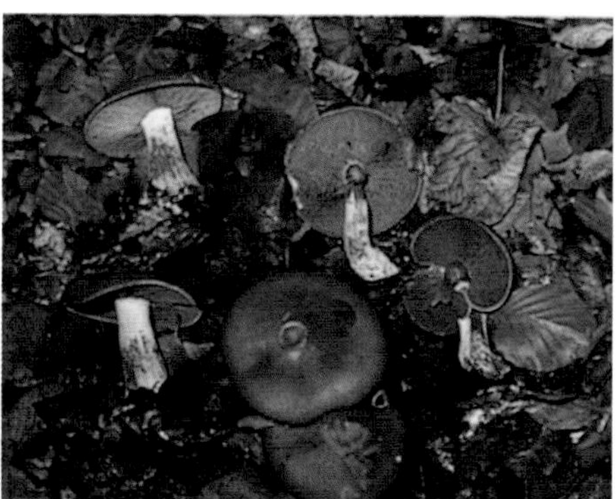

Large, violet to lilac fruitbodies appearing in late autumn and winter.

Cap 2¾–6 in/7–15 cm in diameter, convex expanding with upturned margin, grey-violet or brownish, smooth. *Gills* sinuate, bright violet then discolouring, very crowded. *Stem* 1½–3 × ⅜–¾ in/4–8 × 1–2 cm, thick and often with a swollen base, bright violet. *Flesh* thick, pale or lilaceous, with a faint fruity smell. *Spore deposit* pale pinkish. *Habitat* among leaf-litter, sometimes forming fairy rings. *Similar species Cortinarius alboviolaceus* develops brown gills, has a cobweb-like veil when young and is inedible. *Edibility* good, often sold in European markets, although some people experience an allergic reaction.

GROUP Mushrooms and Toadstools
FAMILY Tricholoma (Tricholomataceae)

 **SEASON** **EDIBILITY** 

HABITAT  On the ground in woodlands or associated with trees

LEPTONIA SERRULATA

Saw Gilled Leptonia *or*
Blue-Toothed Leptonia

The most common of the blue *Leptonia* species, with a black, saw-like gill-edge.

Cap 3/8–1 1/4 in/1–3.5 cm in diameter, convex then expanding to flat with a wavy margin, dark bluish black, with small scales especially at the centre, dry. *Gills* adnate, pale blue then greyish pink with a black edge. *Stem* 3/4–2 × 1/16–3/16 in/2–5 × 0.2–0.4 cm, slender, paler than cap, with dark bluish grey fibrils, and a white, hairy base. *Flesh* pale, brittle. *Spore deposit* pink. *Habitat* fairly common in grassland. *Similar species L. euchroa* is bright violaceous and grows on dead wood, while *L. lampropus* has a grey-brown cap; both inedible. *Edibility* inedible, with an unpleasant taste.

GROUP Mushrooms and Toadstools
FAMILY Entoloma (Entolomataceae)

SEASON 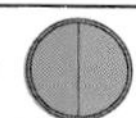 **EDIBILITY** 

HABITAT  On the ground in grassland or open spaces

LEUCOAGARICUS NAUCINUS

Smooth Lepiota

A fleshy grassland fungus, differing from the true mushrooms in having gills which remain white.

Cap 2–4 in/5–10 cm in diameter, broadly convex to flattened, dry, pure white and smooth. *Gills* free, white, broad, crowded. *Stem* 2–3 × 3/16–3/8 in/5–8 × 0.5–1 cm, short and stocky, smooth, white, bearing a white, membranous ring on the upper region. *Flesh* thick, white, firm. *Spore deposit* white. *Habitat* among grass, especially on lawns. *Similar species* this species is easily confused with the true mushrooms (*Agaricus* species), which differ in having gills which darken. Check first with a spore print before attempting to eat. *Edibility* **poisonous**, causing stomach upsets.

GROUP Mushrooms and Toadstools
FAMILY Mushroom and Lepiota (Agaricaceae)

SEASON 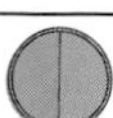 **EDIBILITY** 

HABITAT  On the ground in grassland or open spaces

LEUCOCOPRINUS CEPAESTIPES

Onion-Stalked Lepiota

A white, tufted mushroom, it is recognized by the swollen stem base. Found during the summer months in warmer regions, it often also occurs in hot-houses all year round.

Cap 1¼–2¾ in/3–7 cm in diameter, bell-shaped but finally expanding with a raised centre and a wavy margin, white, radially ridged, but covered with small, powdery scales. *Gills* free, whitish, crowded. *Stem* 2–4 × ⅛–3⁄16 in/5–1 × 0.3–0.5 cm, slender but with a swollen base (up to 1.5 cm across), white bruising yellowish brown, somewhat powdery, and bearing a small, thin ring on the upper region. *Flesh* thin, white, soft. *Spore deposit* white. *Habitat* among grass or leaf-litter. *Similar species L. brebissonii* is smaller, has a black spot in the centre of the cap and a non-swollen stem base; inedible. *Edibility* **possibly poisonous.**

GROUP Mushrooms and Toadstools
FAMILY Mushroom and Lepiota (Agaricaceae)

SEASON  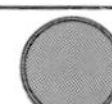 **EDIBILITY** 

HABITAT  On the ground in grassland or open spaces

LYCOPERDON PERLATUM

Common Puffball *or* Gem-Studded Puffball

A common species characterized by the surface which bears numerous conical spines, and in opening by a pore at the top.

Fruitbody 1¼–3 in/3–8 cm high, ¾–2¼ in/2–6 cm in diameter, club-shaped, with a stem-like base, upper part rounded, whitish at first, finally pale brown, opening by a small pore at the top. *Outer layer* composed of short, pyramidal spines each surrounded by a ring of smaller warts. *Inner tissue* white, becoming olive-brown as the spores develop. *Sterile base* firm, spongy, composed of small cells. *Habitat* woodland and pastures. *Similar species L. foetidum* is darker, with groups of blackish brown spines. *L. pedicellatum* has spines 1⁄16 in/0.1–0.2 cm long, often in groups convergent at their tips; both are edible. *Edibility* edible when young and still white inside.

GROUP Puffballs and allies
FAMILY Puffball (Lycoperdaceae)

SEASON 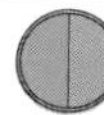 **EDIBILITY** 

HABITAT  On the ground in woodlands or associated with trees

LYCOPERDON PYRIFORME

Stump Puffball *or* Pear-Shaped Puffball

A common species distinguished by the clustered, pear-shaped fruitbodies.

Fruitbody 1½–3 in/4–8 cm high, ¾–1½ in/2–4 cm across the upper part, pear-shaped, whitish becoming pale brown, with white, branching cord-like mycelium at the base. *Surface* scurfy at first, with tiny warts and granules which are soon lost, leaving a smooth inner wall. *Inner wall* thin, papery, opening by a small, irregular pore at the top. *Fertile tissue* at first white, soon greenish yellow and finally olive-brown, with a large central sterile column. *Sterile base* spongy, composed of small cells. *Habitat* in clusters on old stumps and logs or attached to buried wood. *Similar species L. lividum* is less pear-shaped, and does not occur on wood; edible. *Edibility* edible while young and still white inside.

GROUP Puffballs
FAMILY Puffball (Lycoperdaceae)

SEASON 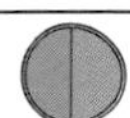 **EDIBILITY** 

HABITAT  On trees, stumps or woody debris

MACROLEPIOTA PROCERA

Parasol Mushroom

A large mushroom, with a woolly cap and a tall stem with movable ring; young fruitbodies resemble drum-sticks.

Cap 3–8 in/8–20 cm in diameter, convex, to flat with a central raised darker area, covered with shaggy, grey-brown scales. *Gills* free, white, broad, very crowded. *Stem* 4–15¾ × ⅜–⅝ in/10–40 × 1–1.5 cm, cylindrical except for a swollen base, covered by fibrous scales, bearing a large double-edged membranous ring in upper region. *Flesh* thick, white, not reddening. *Spore deposit* white. *Habitat* in groups, in meadows and grassy woodland. *Similar species M. gracilenta* has much smaller, indistinct scales on the cap; edible. *M. rhacodes* (see p. 49) has reddening flesh; inedible. *Edibility* one of the best edible species.

GROUP Mushrooms and Toadstools
FAMILY Mushroom and Lepiota (Agaricaceae)

SEASON 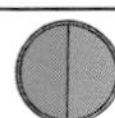 **EDIBILITY** 

HABITAT  On the ground in woodlands or associated with trees

MACROLEPIOTA RHACODES

Shaggy Parasol

A fleshy mushroom with a coarsely scaly cap; bruises reddish.

Cap 2¾–4¾ in/7–12 cm in diameter, convex to flat, pale clay brown, with surface breaking up into large, fibrous scales, except at the centre. *Gills* free, white, broad, very crowded. *Stem* 4–6 × ⅜–1 in/10–15 × 1–2.5 cm, thick and expanding towards the base, smooth, off-white but soon bruising, bearing a large, double-edged, movable ring. *Flesh* thick, white discolouring saffron-red when broken. *Spore deposit* white. *Habitat* in small groups, usually on disturbed soil, at edge of woods or in gardens. *Similar species* in North America, *Chlorophyllum molybdites* is similar but has greenish gills and spore deposit, and the flesh does not discolour reddish; poisonous; *Edibility* edible, can cause an allergic reaction.

GROUP Mushrooms and Toadstools
FAMILY Mushroom and Lepiota (Agaricaceae)

SEASON 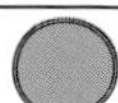 **EDIBILITY** 

HABITAT  On the ground in woodlands or associated with trees

MARASMIUS OREADES

Fairy Ring Champignon

An unpopular species with gardeners owing to its habit of forming extensive fairy rings which last for many years.

Cap ¾–2 in/2–5 cm in diameter, bell-shaped, finally expanding with a wavy margin, pale rusty brown but drying much paler, dry, smooth. *Gills* adnexed, white, broad, widely spaced. *Stem* ¾–2¾ × 1/16–3/16 in/2–7 × 0.2–0.4 cm, thin, tough, similarly coloured to cap, dry. *Flesh* thin, white, with a smell recalling hay. *Spore deposit* white. *Habitat* growing in large numbers in grassland, especially on lawns where it frequently forms extensive, perennial fairy rings. *Similar species* a distinctive species but sometimes growing with the poisonous, white *Clitocybe* species which have decurrent, crowded gills. Take care when collecting this species. *Edibility* edible and good, used in stews and casseroles.

GROUP Mushrooms and Toadstools
FAMILY Tricholoma (Tricholomataceae)

SEASON 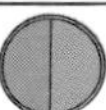 **EDIBILITY** 

HABITAT  On the ground in grassland or open spaces

GROUP Mushrooms and Toadstools
FAMILY Tricholoma (Tricholomataceae)

SEASON  **EDIBILITY** 

HABITAT  On trees, stumps or woody debris

MARASMIUS ROTULA

Little Wheel Toadstool *or* Pinwheel Marasmius

A tiny, membranous toadstool, growing in large numbers on fallen twigs, with widely spaced gills joined by a collar.

Cap 3/16–3/8 in/0.5–1 cm in diameter, strongly convex with a sunken centre, white to pale yellowish brown, smooth and dry, with, radial grooves. *Gills* broadly attached to a circular collar around the stem apex, white, widely spaced. *Stem* ¾–1½ × 1/16 in/2–4 × 0.1–0.2 cm, wiry, at first yellow soon blackish brown from the base upwards, smooth. *Flesh* membranous, white. *Spore deposit* white. *Habitat* growing on fallen twigs of deciduous trees. *Similar species M. epiphyllus* lacks a collar at the stem apex, while *M. capillaripes* grows on oak leaves; both inedible. *Edibility* edible but worthless.

GROUP Mushrooms and Toadstools
FAMILY Tricholoma (Tricholomataceae)

SEASON  **EDIBILITY** 

HABITAT  On trees, stumps or woody debris

MEGACOLLYBIA PLATYPHYLLA

Broad-Gilled Agaric *or* Platterful Mushroom

A large mushroom characterized by the grey, streaky cap, and the white mycelial cords attached to the stem base.

Cap 2–4 in/5–10 cm in diameter, convex soon becoming flattened, greyish brown, dry, with conspicuous radial streaks. *Gills* adnexed, white, often very broad and easily splitting, well spaced. *Stem* 3–4¾ × ⅜–¾ in/8–12 × 1–2 cm, cylindrical and robust, white, fibrous, arising from conspicuous, white, branching mycelial cords. *Flesh* thin, white. *Spore deposit* white. *Habitat* on dead fallen wood and stumps of deciduous trees. *Similar species* this species differs from *Tricholoma* species by always growing on wood. *Edibility* not recommended, with a bitter taste and can cause stomach upsets.

MELANOLEUCA MELALEUCA

Changeable Melanoleuca

A fleshy mushroom, with a dark brown cap and brown, fibrillose stem, contrasting with white, crowded gills.

Cap 1¼–4 in/3–10 cm in diameter, soon flattening but retaining a knob-like centre, smoky brown drying paler, smooth. *Gills* sinuate, broad. *Stem* 1¼–3 × ⅜–¾ in/3–8 × 1–2 cm, same length as cap diameter, fibrous, often twisted, whitish, with dark brown, vertical fibrils. *Flesh* pale, greyish, thick, lacking a smell. *Spore deposit* white. *Habitat* under leafy trees, although this species may also be found in meadows or even on lawns. *Similar species M. cognata* is yellowish brown, *M. grammopodia* is large and robust, and *M. brevipes* has a short stem; all inedible. *Edibility* edible but not recommended.

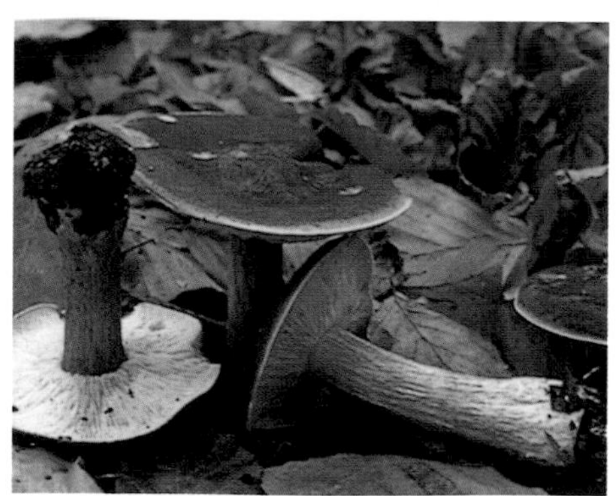

GROUP Mushrooms and Toadstools
FAMILY Tricholoma (Tricholomataceae)

SEASON 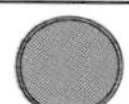 **EDIBILITY** 

HABITAT  On the ground in woodlands or associated with trees

MORCHELLA ELATA

Black Morel

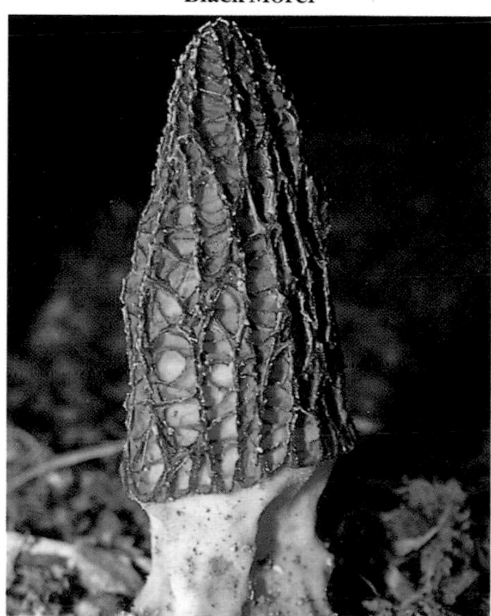

A woodland species with a narrow honeycomb-patterned conical cap.

Cap ¾–2¼ in/2–6 cm high, ¾–1½ in/2–4 cm wide, separated from stem by a groove, hollow, conical, with regular, yellowish brown pits separated by grey or blackish vertical ribs and paler horizontal ribs. *Stem* 1½–3 × ¾–1½ in/4–8 × 2–4 cm, cylindrical, hollow, whitish, the surface coarsely mealy. *Flesh* thin, brittle, whitish. *Spore deposit* ochraceous. *Habitat* especially coniferous woodlands, burnt ground. *Similar species M. conica* has vertical, parallel ribs which are not darker than the pits; edible. *Edibility* edible after cooking.

GROUP Cup Fungi
FAMILY Morel (Morchellaceae)

SEASON  **EDIBILITY** 

HABITAT  On the ground in grassland or open spaces

MORCHELLA ESCULENTA

Common Morel *or* Yellow Morel

A robust, club-shaped species. *Cap* 2–4 in/5–10 cm high, 1½–2¼ in/4–6 cm wide, separated from the stalk by narrow groove, subglobose, oval or bluntly conical, yellowish brown, honeycomb-like. *Stem* 1¼–2¼ × ¾–1½ in/3–6 × 2–4 cm, often swollen at base, irregularly ribbed, whitish, minutely scurfy, hollow. *Flesh* brittle, thin, whitish. *Spore deposit* ochraceous. *Habitat* open scrub or waste ground, chalky soil. *Similar species M. elata* (see page 51); *M. hortensis* has a more elongated, conical cap and parallel ribs. Both edible. *Edibility* excellent edible species, but should never be eaten raw.

GROUP Cup Fungi
FAMILY Morel (Morchellaceae)

SEASON  **EDIBILITY** 

HABITAT  On the ground in grassland or open spaces

MORCHELLA SEMILIBERA

Half Free Morel

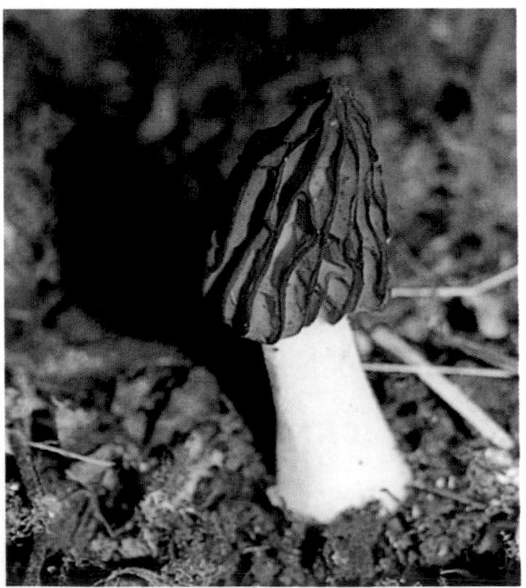

A distinctive, spring-fruiting species. *Cap* ⅝–1½ in/1.5–4 cm high, ⅝–1¼ in/1.5–3 cm wide, conical, free from the stem for the lower half of its length, with yellowish brown fertile pits separated by irregular, dark brown or blackish ribs. *Stem* 2¼–4 × ⅜–¾ in/6–10 × 1–2 cm, hollow, often tall, usually thickened towards the base, whitish to cream, surface scurfy. *Flesh* thin, brittle, whitish. *Habitat* damp soil in woods, hedges or on waste ground. *Similar species M. elata* (see page 51); edible. *Edibility* a good edible species, but should always be cooked.

GROUP Cup Fungi
FAMILY Morel (Morchellaceae)

SEASON  **EDIBILITY** 

HABITAT  On the ground in grassland or open spaces

MYCENA HAEMATOPUS

Bleeding Mycena

A dark, clustered elf cap, growing on rotting wood, which releases a dark red juice when the stem is broken.

Cap $\frac{3}{4}$–$1\frac{1}{4}$ in/2–3 cm in diameter, bell-shaped to convex, dark reddish brown, with radiating streaks, dry. *Gills* adnexed, whitish, staining reddish brown, moderately spaced. *Stem* $1\frac{1}{4}$–3 × $\frac{1}{16}$–$\frac{1}{8}$ in/3–8 × 0.2–0.3 cm, cylindrical or flattened, reddish brown, with a hairy base. *Flesh* thin, reddish, which in the stem releases a dark blood-red liquid when broken. *Spore deposit* white. *Habitat* common growing on rotting wood. *Similar species M. sanguinolenta* also releases a red juice when broken but grows on the ground, among moss, and is much more slender; inedible. *Edibility* worthless.

GROUP Mushrooms and Toadstools
FAMILY Tricholoma (Tricholomataceae)

SEASON  **EDIBILITY** 

HABITAT  On trees, stumps or woody debris

MYCENA INCLINATA

Gregarious Elf Cap

A tufted elf cap, growing on oak-stumps, with a reddish brown stem base.

Cap $\frac{3}{8}$–$1\frac{1}{2}$ in/1–4 cm in diameter, bell-shaped, dark yellowish brown, smooth, radially striated, with a toothed margin. *Gills* adnate, whitish, narrow, crowded. *Stem* 2–3 × $\frac{1}{16}$–$\frac{1}{8}$ in/5–8 × 0.2–0.3 cm, cylindrical, greyish darkening to yellow and finally dark reddish brown towards the base. *Flesh* thin, brittle, with an odour of rancid oil. *Spore deposit* white. *Habitat* tufted on oak-stumps. *Similar species* the inedible *M. galericulata* with a brownish stem base. *Edibility* inedible.

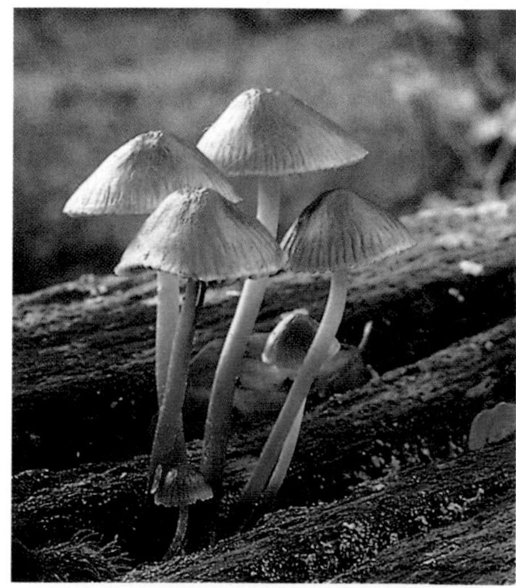

GROUP Mushrooms and Toadstools
FAMILY Tricholoma (Tricholomataceae)

 **SEASON**  **EDIBILITY** 

HABITAT 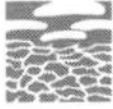 On trees, stumps or woody debris

MYCENA LEPTOCEPHALA

Nitrous Mycena

A very common *Mycena* species, with an alkaline smell and grey colours.

Cap ¾–1¼ in/2–3 cm in diameter, bell-shaped, greyish brown, paler at the margin, radially striated. *Gills* adnate, greyish, moderately spaced. *Stem* 2–2¾ × 1/16 in/5–7 × 0.1–0.2 cm, slender, cylindrical, hollow and brittle, similarly coloured to cap or paler. *Flesh* thin, grey, watery, brittle, with a strong alkaline smell. *Spore deposit* white. *Habitat* solitary on soil among short grass, and often pine-needles. *Similar species* the Stump Mycena *(M. alcalina)* is similar but forms small tufts on rotting woods; inedible. *Edibility* inedible.

GROUP Mushrooms and Toadstools
FAMILY Tricholoma (Tricholomataceae)

SEASON  **EDIBILITY** 

HABITAT  On the ground in grassland or open spaces

MYCENA PURA

Lilac Mycena *or* Pink Mycena

One of the larger *Mycena* species, distinguished by the pink to lilac colour, lack of a dark edge to the gills, and a smell that reminds one of radishes.

Cap ¾–2¼ in/2–6 cm in diameter, convex to bell-shaped, finally expanding and becoming flattened, pink or lilac, often drying paler, smooth, striated at the margin. *Stem* 1¼–3 × 3/16–⅜ in/3–8 × 0.4–1 cm, slender but rigid, slightly thicker towards the base, similarly coloured to the cap or slightly paler, shining, whitish-downy at the base. *Flesh* thin, pinkish, with a smell of radish. *Spore deposit* white. *Habitat* among leaf-litter in deciduous woodland, especially under beech. *Similar species M. pelianthina* is also found in beech woods but has gills with a dark violaceous edge; poisonous. *Edibility* **poisonous.**

GROUP Mushrooms and Toadstools
FAMILY Tricholoma (Tricholomataceae)

SEASON  **EDIBILITY** 

HABITAT  On the ground in woodlands or associated with trees

NOLANEA SERICEA
Silky Nolanea

A pink-spored toadstool, commonly found on lawns throughout the autumn months.

Cap 3/4–1 1/2 in/2–4 cm in diameter, convex then expanded with a wavy margin, dark brown and finely striate when moist but drying much paler and becoming shiny-silky. *Gills* adnexed, pale grey becoming progressively pink, moderately crowded. *Stem* 3/4–2 × 1/8 in/2–5 × 0.2–0.3 cm, slender, fibrous, greyish brown. *Flesh* thin, greyish, watery, with a strong smell of meal. *Spore deposit* pink. *Habitat* common, scattered among short grass and frequently encountered on lawns. *Similar species* there are a number of slender *Nolanea* species growing in grassland, but most are less common and require detailed examination under the microscope for identification. *Edibility* inedible.

GROUP Mushrooms and Toadstools
FAMILY Entoloma (Entolomataceae)

SEASON 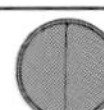 **EDIBILITY** 

HABITAT  On the ground in grassland or open spaces

NYCTALIS PARASITICA
Pick-A-Back Toadstool

A small, slender, pale toadstool, growing in groups on old, rotting fruitbodies of brittle-gills and milk-caps.

Cap 3/8–1 1/4 in/1–3 cm in diameter, bell-shaped then expanding, pale lilac-grey, smooth with a silky surface. *Gills* broadly adnate, white to brownish, often thick and distorted, well spaced. *Stem* 5/8–1 1/2 × 1/16–3/16 in/1.5–4 × 0.2–0.4 cm, cylindrical, greyish white. *Flesh* thin, white, firm. *Spore deposit* white. *Habitat* on rotting brittle-gills (*Russula* species) or milk-caps (*Lactarius* species). *Similar species Collybia tuberosa* (inedible) and related species grow on similar substrates but have well-developed gills. The stem of *C. tuberosa* originates from a small brown tuber (sclerotium). *Edibility* worthless.

GROUP Mushrooms and Toadstools
FAMILY Tricholoma (Tricholomataceae)

SEASON  **EDIBILITY** 

HABITAT  On other fungi

OTIDEA ONOTICA

Lemon Peel Fungus

An ear-shaped species distinguished by its ochraceous, pink-tinged fruitbodies.

Cup 1½–4 in/4–10 cm high, 1¼–2¼ in/3–6 cm wide, elongated on one side and irregularly rabbit-ear shaped with short, indistinct stalk. *Fertile inner surface* smooth, ochraceous, distinctly tinged with pink, drying with a more pronounced pink tint. *Outer surface* similarly coloured, drying ochraceous, finely scurfy. *Flesh* thin, whitish, with no distinctive smell. *Habitat* in leaf-litter in deciduous or mixed woodland, often in clusters. *Similar species* species of *Flavoscypha* may be similar in form, but are brighter yellow and lack pink tints; inedible. *Edibility* inedible.

GROUP Cup Fungi
FAMILY Large Cup Fungi (Pezizaceae)

SEASON  **EDIBILITY** 

HABITAT  On the ground in woodlands or associated with trees

OUDEMANSIELLA RADICATA

Rooting Shank

A large, common and conspicuous mushroom found in the autumn, with a shiny, brown cap and a deeply rooting stem.

Cap 2–4 in/5–10 cm in diameter, convex soon flattened and forming an upturned, wavy margin, yellowish brown to dark brown, slimy when moist, with a wrinkled centre. *Gills* adnate, white, thick and broad, moderately spaced. *Stem* 2–8 × 3⁄16–3⁄8 in/5–20 × 0.5–1 cm, rather brittle, white at the apex, brownish below and expanding slightly downwards to form a long, underground root-like extension. *Flesh* thick, white. *Spore deposit* white. *Habitat* apparently growing on the ground but attached to underground tree roots, especially of beech. *Similar species O. pudens* is less common and has a dry, velvety cap and stem; inedible. *Edibility* edible.

GROUP Mushrooms and Toadstools
FAMILY Tricholoma (Tricholomataceae)

SEASON 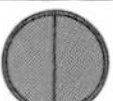 **EDIBILITY** 

HABITAT  On trees, stumps or woody debris

PANAEOLUS SPHINCTRINUS

Grey Mottle-Gill

A common, slender mottle-gill with a dark grey stem and scales on the cap margin.

Cap ¾–1¼ in/2–3 cm in diameter, bell-shaped, dark grey, smooth, often with a fringe of tiny, white scales on the veil. *Gills* adnate, blackish brown, mottled, crowded. *Stem* 2¾ 4¾ × 1⁄16–⅛ in/7–12 × 0.2–0.3 cm, tall and slender, dark greyish to blackish, finely powdery, *Flesh* thin, grey, firm. *Habitat* on cowpats in fields. *Similar species P. campanulatus* has a reddish brown cap and stem, usually found on horse dung; mildly poisonous. *Edibility* inedible, **possibly poisonous.**

GROUP Mushrooms and Toadstools
FAMILY Ink-cap (Coprinaceae)

SEASON  **EDIBILITY** 

HABITAT 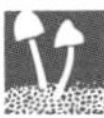 On dung or enriched soil

PANELLUS STIPTICUS

Styptic Fungus *or* Luminescent Panellus

A small, brown, tough oyster mushroom, with very crowded narrow gills, which emit a greenish light in the dark.

Cap ⅜–1¼ in/1–3 cm in diameter, kidney-shaped, pale buffy brown, dry, scurfy to hairy. *Gills* adnate, pinkish brown, very narrow, crowded. *Stem* 3⁄16–⅝ × 3⁄16–⅜ in/0.5–1.5 × 0.5–1 cm, very short, strongly off-centre to lateral, broadest at the point of attachment to the cap, flattened, very pale brown, hairy. *Flesh* thin, tough, brown, with a bitter taste. *Spore deposit* white. *Habitat* clustered, on logs and stumps. *Similar species* this species is easily confused with *Crepidotus* species, and a spore print is required to be certain of identification. *Edibility* inedible, bitter and **possibly toxic.**

GROUP Mushrooms and Toadstools
FAMILY Tricholoma (Tricholomataceae)

SEASON  **EDIBILITY** 

HABITAT  On trees, stumps or woody debris

PAXILLUS INVOLUTUS
Brown Roll-Rim *or* Poison Paxillus

A very common, large species with brown gills which feel slimy when squashed.

Cap 1½–8 in/4–20 cm in diameter, convex to flat, soon depressed, brown, dry although slimy when wet, with a ridged margin inrolled. *Gills* decurrent, olive-green – yellowish, bruising brown, forked and crowded, and easily detached from the cap. *Stem* 1½–2¾ × ⅜–¾ in/4–7 × 1–2 cm, firm, yellowish brown, bruising reddish brown, smooth. *Flesh* yellowish, thick, soft. *Spore deposit* clay-brown. *Habitat* on the ground in mixed woods or heathland, often with birch. *Similar species P. rubicundulus* has a scaly cap and yellowish gills, *P. filamentosus* does not bruise reddish brown; both poisonous. *Edibility* **poisonous.**

GROUP Boletes
FAMILY Paxillus (Paxillaceae)

SEASON 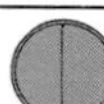 **EDIBILITY** 

HABITAT  On the ground in woodlands or associated with trees

PEZIZA VESICULOSA
Early Cup Fungus *or* Bladder Cup

Forms clusters of large, thick-fleshed, cup-shaped fruitbodies on manured soil. *Fruitbody* 1¼–4 in/3–10 cm across, cup-shaped with a strongly inrolled, crenulate margin. *Inner surface* pale yellowish brown, usually wrinkled, or blistered in large specimens. *Outer surface* paler, coarsely scurfy. *Flesh* thick, brittle, pale fawn. *Habitat* on rich soil or manure, often in large clusters; common. *Similar species* other species of *Peziza* are less massive and have thinner flesh, but, in order to distinguish small specimens of *P. vesiculosa,* microscopic examination may be required. *Edibility* inedible.

GROUP Cup Fungi
FAMILY Large Cup Fungi (Pezizaceae)

SEASON  **EDIBILITY** 

HABITAT 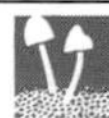 On dung or enriched soil

PHAEOLEPIOTA AUREA

Golden False Pholiota

A large, distinctive species of parks and roadsides, with a powdery, orange-brown cap and striate, funnel-shaped ring.

Cap 4–9 in/10–25 cm in diameter, convex, orange-brown, surface scurfy or powdery, the margin often fringed with tooth-like remnants of the veil. *Gills* adnexed, almost free, pale orange-yellow. *Stem* 4–8 × 1¼–1½ in/ 10–20 × 3–4 cm, stout, pale orange-brown or yellowish brown, sheathed below and bearing a large, membranous ring which is powdery and conspicuously striated on the underside. *Flesh* whitish, without any distinctive smell. *Spore deposit* ochraceous brown. *Habitat* in parks and open woodland, often in clusters. *Similar species* not likely to be confused with any other specimen. *Edibility* edible, but not recommended.

GROUP Mushrooms and Toadstools
FAMILY Cortinarius (Cortinariaceae)

SEASON  **EDIBILITY** 

HABITAT  On the ground in woodlands or associated with trees

PHAEOLUS SCHWEINITZII

Large Pine Polyporus *or* Dye Polypore

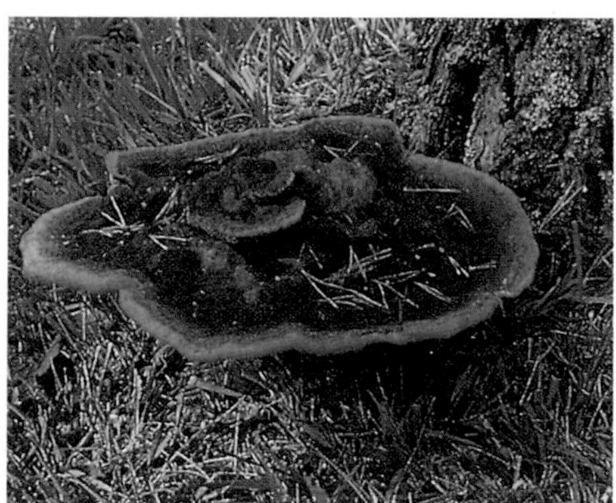

This centrally stalked, bracket fungus forms large, plate-like caps with a sulphur-yellow margin and a brown flesh.

Cap 3–12 in/8–30 cm in diameter, flat and plate-like, with concentric orange zones and a dark reddish brown centre, felty, with a sulphur-yellow margin; blackish on weathering. *Tubes* up to ⅜ in/1 cm long, brown, brittle; *pores* 2–5 per 1/16 in/0.1 cm, often splitting and maze-like, greenish yellow discolouring brown. *Stem* 1¼–3 × ¾–2 in/3–8 × 2–5 cm, short, solid, dark rusty brown. *Flesh* ¾–1¼ in/2–3 cm thick, brown, soft at first becoming fibrous and brittle. *Spore deposit* white. *Habitat* on dead or living coniferous wood. *Similar species Coltricia* species have a central stem and brown flesh, but are smaller and thinner; inedible. *Edibility* inedible.

GROUP Bracket Fungi
FAMILY Brown Polypore (Hymenochaetaceae)

SEASON 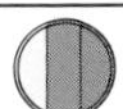 **EDIBILITY** 

HABITAT  On trees, stumps or woody debris

PHALLUS IMPUDICUS
Common Stinkhorn

A common species in woodlands located by its nauseous odour.

Egg 1¼–1½ in/3–4 cm in diameter, ball-shaped, bearing root-like cords at the base, white, smooth and gelatinous, rupturing to release the stalk. *Stalk* up to 8 in/20 cm high, ⅝–1 in/1.5–2.5 cm in diameter, cylindrical, white, spongy and hollow. *Gleba* attached to stalk apex, conical, covered initially by a stinking green-brown slime. *Habitat* leaf-litter. *Similar species P. ravenelii* has a yellowish stalk and a pinkish egg; inedible. *Edibility* the unopened egg is said to be edible.

GROUP Stinkhorns
FAMILY Phallaceae

SEASON  **EDIBILITY** 

HABITAT  On the ground in woodlands or associated with trees

PHOLIOTA AURIVELLA
Golden Pholiota

A large, brown-gilled mushroom, growing on the upper branches of living trees, with a slimy scaly, yellow cap and a dry stem.

Cap 3–4¾ in/8–12 cm in diameter, bright yellow with a darker centre, slimy, and bearing scattered, flat, slimy, reddish brown scales. *Gills* adnate, yellowish then rusty brown, crowded. *Stem* 3½–6 × ⅜–⅝ in/9–15 × 1–1.5 cm, cylindrical, dry, yellowish brown becoming much darker at the base, bearing a small, fibrous ring towards the apex. *Flesh* thick, pale yellow. *Spore deposit* rusty brown. *Habitat* small clumps on trees, especially beech and maple, often on upper branches. *Similar species P. squarrosa* has a dry cap, while *P. adiposa* has a slimy cap and stem; both inedible. *Edibility* inedible.

GROUP Mushrooms and Toadstools
FAMILY Stropharia (Strophariaceae)

SEASON  **EDIBILITY** 

HABITAT  On trees, stumps or woody debris

PHOLIOTA HIGHLANDENSIS

Charcoal Pholiota

A very common toadstool on burnt ground and charred wood, distinguished by the slimy cap and reddish brown gills.

Cap 1¼–2 in/3–5 cm in diameter, convex becoming flattened with a wavy margin, chestnut-brown becoming paler on drying, slightly sticky, smooth. *Gills* adnate, clay-brown, crowded. *Stem* ¾–2 × ⅛–3⁄16 in/2–5 × 0.3–0.5 cm, short, yellowish brown, paler at the apex, with small fibre-scales. *Flesh* thin, pale, firm. *Spore deposit* cinnamon-brown. *Habitat* on burnt ground or burnt stumps. *Similar species P. spumosa* has a slimy, yellowish cap, and grows in conifer woods; inedible. *Edibility* inedible.

GROUP Mushrooms and Toadstools
FAMILY Stropharia (Strophariaceae)

SEASON  **EDIBILITY** 

HABITAT  On burnt ground or on burnt wood

PIPTOPORUS BETULINUS

Razor-Strop Fungus *or* Birch Polypore

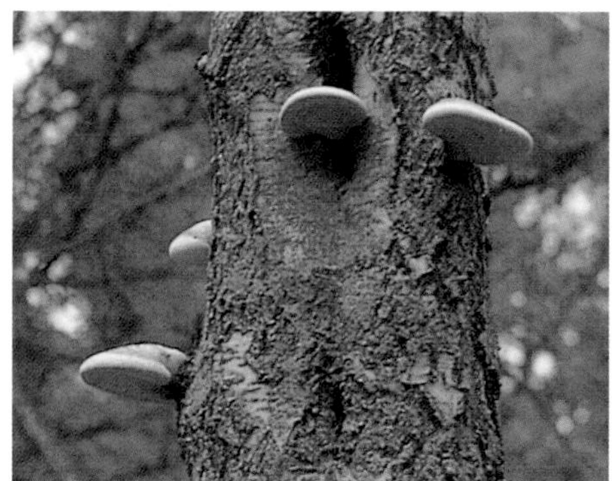

Always found in large numbers on birch trees, and easily recognized by the smooth, rounded caps.

Cap 2–8 in/5–20 cm in diameter, round, hoof-shaped with a narrow, lateral attachment to the host; surface at first white soon becoming greyish brown, not zoned, smooth, with a broadly rounded edge and an inrolled margin. *Tubes* up to ⅜ in/1 cm long, white, developing late; *pores* small, 3–4 per 1⁄16 in/0.1 cm, whitish discolouring brownish. *Flesh* up to 1¼ in/3 cm thick, pure white and corky. *Spore deposit* white. *Habitat* on trunks of living and dead birch trees. *Similar species* always confined to birch trees, this species is unlikely to be confused. *Edibility* inedible.

GROUP Bracket Fungi
FAMILY Poroid Bracket (Coriolaceae)

SEASON 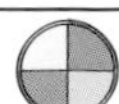 **EDIBILITY** 

HABITAT 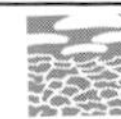 On trees, stumps or woody debris

PLEUROCYBELLA PORRIGENS
Angel's Wings

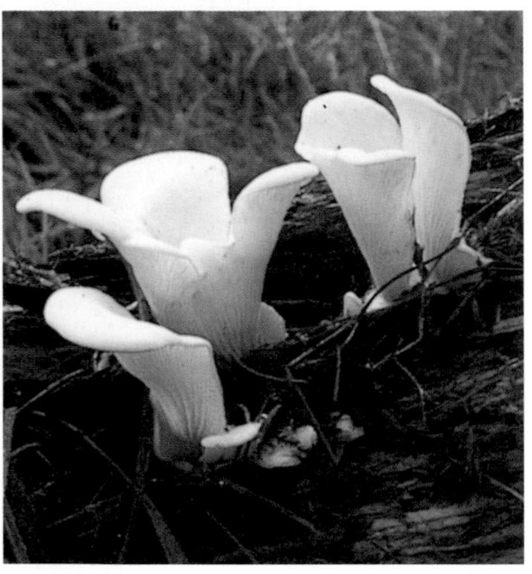

Often forms large numbers of white clusters, with fan-shaped fruitbodies, on coniferous stumps and debris.

Cap 3/4–4 in/2–10 cm in diameter, fan-shaped, often erect, pure white, dry and smooth, with an incurved margin. *Gills* decurrent, creamy white, narrow, and very crowded. *Stem* none or very reduced. *Flesh* thin, white, brittle. *Spore deposit* white. *Habitat* on rotting coniferous wood, prefers colder regions. *Similar species* this species is thinner-fleshed than most of the true oyster mushrooms. *Edibility* edible.

GROUP Mushrooms and Toadstools
FAMILY Tricholoma (Tricholomataceae)

SEASON  **EDIBILITY** 

HABITAT  On trees, stumps or woody debris

PLEUROTUS DRYINUS
Veiled Oyster

A large oyster mushroom, with a ring on the stem and yellowing gills.

Cap 2 3/4–5 1/2 in/7–14 cm in diameter, strongly convex, whitish, with a felty surface, dry, sometimes cracking. *Gills* decurrent, white drying yellowish, moderately crowded. *Stem* 3/4–2 × 3/8–1 1/4 in/2–5 × 1–3 cm, off-centre, short, whitish, solid, with a thin, membranous, greyish ring which disintegrates. *Flesh* thick, white, with an aromatic odour. *Spore deposit* white. *Habitat* on deciduous trees. *Similar species* other oyster mushrooms form clusters, and lack a ring on the stem. *Edibility* edible when young.

GROUP Bracket Fungi
FAMILY Lentinus and Oyster Cap (Lentinaceae)

SEASON  **EDIBILITY** 

HABITAT 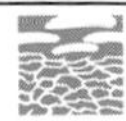 On trees, stumps or woody debris

PLEUROTUS OSTREATUS
Oyster Mushroom

A well-known edible species with a greyish brown cap and lateral attachment.

Cap 2–5½ in/5–14 cm in diameter, shell-shaped, semi-circular, gradually expanding and becoming flattened with a wavy margin, whitish to greyish brown, blue-grey or deep violet, smooth and dry. *Gills* decurrent, white, broad, and moderately crowded. *Stem* none, or very short and laterally attached, thick and solid. *Flesh* thick, white, with a pleasant "mushroom" odour. *Spore deposit* very pale lilac. *Habitat* on stumps and trunks of frondose trees, especially beech. *Similar species* there are many varieties, mostly based upon cap colour. *P. pulmonarius* is thinner and has a whitish cap, while *P. cornucopiae* has gills which form a network over the top of the stem; both edible. *Edibility* excellent.

GROUP Bracket Fungi
FAMILY Lentinus and Oyster Cap (Lentinaceae)

SEASON 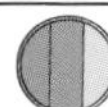 **EDIBILITY** 

HABITAT  On trees, stumps or woody debris

PLUTEUS CERVINUS
Fawn Pluteus

One of the most common toadstools, recognized by the crowded, pink gills which are free from the stem apex.

Cap 1¼–4¾ in/3–12 cm in diameter, convex soon becoming flattened, greyish brown or darker, smooth but with radiating, darker striations, dry. *Gills* free, white but becoming salmon-pink as the spores develop, thin, very crowded. *Stem* 2–4 × 3/16–3/8 in/5–10 × 0.5–1 cm, cylindrical, solid, white, with fine, blackish brown fibres. *Flesh* thin, white. *Spore deposit* salmon-pink. *Habitat* common, on old stumps, fallen wood and sawdust. *Similar species* in North America, *P. magnus* is stouter; *P. atromarginatus* has a dark gill edge. *Edibility* said to be edible when very young but soon decaying, not recommended.

GROUP Mushrooms and Toadstools
FAMILY Pluteus (Pluteaceae)

SEASON  **EDIBILITY** 

HABITAT  On trees, stumps or woody debris

POLYPORUS SQUAMOSUS
Dryad's Saddle

This polypore forms plate-like, yellowish caps on deciduous trees.

Cap 4–20 in/10–50 cm in diameter, laterally to almost centrally attached to the stem, kidney-shaped, yellowish brown with blackish brown, pointed scales in concentric zones, and a thin, downturned margin. *Tubes* decurrent, up to 5⁄16 in/0.7 cm long; *pores* large and angular, 1–2 per 1⁄16 in/0.1 cm, cream-coloured. *Stem* 1¼–4 × ⅜–2 in/3–10 × 1–5 cm, cylindrical, solid, pale above, with a black velvety base. *Flesh* ¾–1½ in/2–4 cm thick, white, with a sweet odour. *Spore deposit* white. *Habitat* on trees. *Similar species P. tuberaster* is smaller, grows from an underground tuber; inedible. *Edibility* said to be edible when young, not recommended.

GROUP Bracket Fungi
FAMILY True Polyporus (Polyporaceae)

SEASON **EDIBILITY**

HABITAT On trees, stumps or woody debris

PSATHYRELLA GRACILIS
Slender Psathyrella

A tall, slender, brittle toadstool distinguished by pink-edged, dark grey gills.

Cap ¾–1¼ in/2–3 cm in diameter, bell-shaped then expanded, brown when moist, drying to greyish brown, smooth, with a striated margin. *Gills* adnate, greyish to black, with a pink edge, narrow, moderately crowded. *Stem* 1¼–4 × ⅛ in/3–10 × 0.2–0.3 cm, slender, tall, white, with a hairy base. *Flesh* thin, watery. *Spore deposit* purplish black. *Habitat* grasslands and woodlands. *Similar species* unlikely to be confused with other species. *Edibility* inedible.

GROUP Mushrooms and Toadstools
FAMILY Ink-cap (Coprinaceae)

SEASON  **EDIBILITY** 

HABITAT 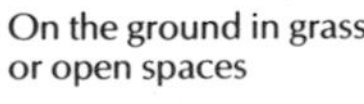 On the ground in grassland or open spaces

PSATHYRELLA HYDROPHILA

Watery Hypholoma *or* Clustered Psathyrella

Grows on rotten wood, and has brown cap and gills, and a white stem.

Cap ¾–2 in/2–5 cm across, expanding, smooth, dark brown when fresh, pale ochre when dry. Margin with white remnants of the veil. *Gills* brown, adnate, crowded. *Stem* 2–2¾ × ⅛–3/16 in/5–7 × 0.3–0.5 cm, white, smooth. *Flesh* whitish, thin, fragile, hollow in the stem. *Spore deposit* dark brown. *Habitat* in dense clusters on stumps and logs of deciduous trees; common. *Similar species P. spadicea* lacks a veil and has pinkish tints in the cap; inedible. *Edibility* inedible.

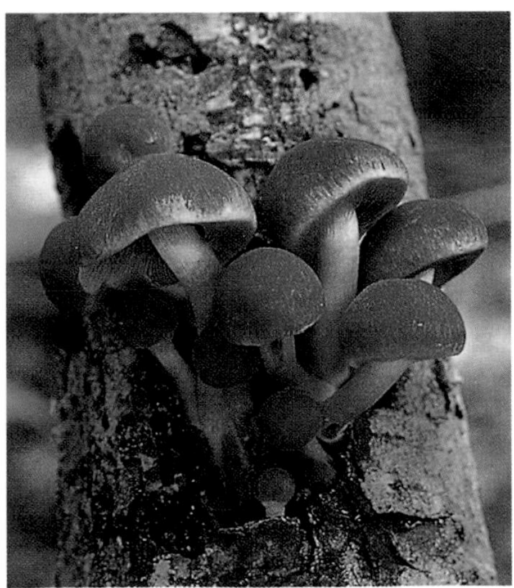

GROUP Mushrooms and Toadstools
FAMILY Ink-cap (Coprinacea)

SEASON  **EDIBILITY** 

HABITAT  On trees, stumps or woody debris

PSILOCYBE SEMILANCEATA

Liberty Cap

A well-known species, owing to its reputation as a "magic mushroom".

Cap ⅜–⅝ in/1–1.5 cm in diameter, narrowly conical with a central, pointed projection, pale yellowish brown, smooth, sticky, with a darker, striated margin. *Gills* adnate, grey-brown to blackish brown. *Stem* 2–3 × ⅛ in/5–8 × 0.2–0.3 cm, slender, cylindrical, paler than cap, base often bruising bluish green. *Flesh* thin, firm. *Spore deposit* purplish black. *Habitat* open grassland. *Similar species P. cyanescens* lacks a point on cap, while *P. fimetaria* grows on dung; both poisonous. *Edibility* **toxic**, causing psychotropic poisoning.

GROUP Mushrooms and Toadstools
FAMILY Stropharia (Strophariaceae)

SEASON  **EDIBILITY** 

HABITAT  On the ground in grassland or open spaces

PYCNOPORUS CINNABARINUS
Cinnabar-Red Polypore

An easily recognized, small bracket fungus, with all parts coloured bright orange-red.

Cap ¾–4 in/2–10 cm in diameter, semicircular with a broad lateral attachment, orange-red discolouring paler in old specimens, smooth or uneven, with a thin, straight margin. *Tubes* 3/16–¼ in/0.4–0.6 cm long; *pores* 2–3 per 1/16 in/0.1 cm, deep orange-red. *Flesh* up to ¾ in/2 cm thick, tough and corky, orange-red, lacking an odour. *Spore deposit* white. *Habitat* on dead wood of both deciduous trees, especially oak, and conifers; sometimes several caps are joined by their sides. *Similar species* the orange-red is so distinctive that it cannot be confused. In southern North America, *P. sanguineus* is found which is usually much thinner; inedible. *Edibility* inedible.

GROUP Bracket fungi
FAMILY Poroid Bracket (Coriolaceae)

SEASON 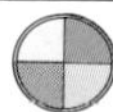 **EDIBILITY** 

HABITAT 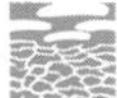 On trees, stumps or woody debris

RAMARIA FORMOSA
Yellow-Tipped Coral Fungus

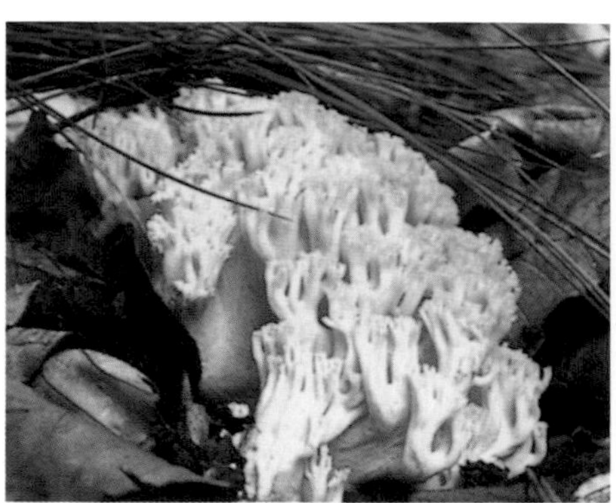

An occasional species that forms large, salmon-pink tufts, with yellow tips.

Fruitbody 2–8 in/5–20 cm in diameter, with dense branching arising from a short but stout basal stalk, salmon-pink with pale yellowish tips, bruising brown. *Flesh* fibrous, pinky brown. *Spore deposit* pale brown. *Habitat* on the ground under conifers. *Similar species R. aurea* does not stain brown on bruising and *R. botrytis* is whitish with red-tipped branches; both poisonous. *Edibility* **poisonous**, known to cause severe stomach upsets.

GROUP Club Fungi
FAMILY Coral Fungi (Ramariaceae)

SEASON  **EDIBILITY** 

HABITAT  On the ground in woodlands or associated with trees

RHIZINA UNDULATA

Pine Fire Fungus *or* Crust-like Cup

Forms distinctive, dark brown, convex fruitbodies having a pale margin and firm flesh, and attached to the substrate by whitish root-like structures.

Fruitbody 1½–4¾ in/4–12 cm across, convex and cushion-like, often lobed and irregular in outline. *Upper surface* undulating, dark chestnut-brown, with a pale, cream margin, smooth. *Underside* cream or pale ochraceous, attached to the substrate by numerous branched, whitish, root-like structures. *Flesh* firm, tough, thick, reddish brown, without a distinctive smell. *Habitat* usually on burnt ground in coniferous woods; causes a disease of conifers known as group dying. *Similar species* unlikely to be confused with other species. *Edibility* inedible.

GROUP Cup Fungi
FAMILY Saddle-cup (Helvellaceae)

SEASON  **EDIBILITY** 

HABITAT  On burnt ground or on burnt wood

ROZITES CAPERATA

Gypsy Mushroom

A large, cream-coloured mushroom, with brown gills, characterized by the conspicuous, membranous ring on the stem.

Cap 2¼–4¾ in/6–12 cm in diameter, con vex then flattened with an upturned, wavy margin, dull straw-yellow, dry, with a hoary-powdery aspect. *Gills* adnate, brown, broad, often vertically wrinkled, crowded. *Stem* 4–6 × ⅜–¾ in/10–15 × 1–2 cm, cylindrical, white to yellowish ochre, with longitudinal striations, and bearing a prominent, white, membranous ring attached to the upper region. *Flesh* thick, white, with a pleasant smell. *Spore deposit* rusty brown. *Habitat* on acidic, sandy soil, under trees, preferring northerly or mountainous localities. *Similar species* closely resembles other *Cortinarius* species, which may be poisonous. *Edibility* said to be good after cooking.

GROUP Mushrooms and Toadstools
FAMILY Cortinarius (Cortinariaceae)

SEASON  **EDIBILITY** 

HABITAT  On the ground in woodlands or associated with trees

RUSSULA EMETICA
Emetic Russula

A bright red *Russula* of coniferous woodland, with a very peppery flesh.

Cap 1¼–2¼ in/3–6 cm in diameter, hard, convex to flat or with a depressed centre, scarlet red to deep blood-red, smooth, sticky, with an obtusely rounded margin. *Gills* adnexed, off-white, broad, spaced. *Stem* 2–3 × ⅜–¾ in/5–8 × 1–2 cm, pure white, brittle. *Flesh* thick, white, with a strongly acrid taste. *Spore deposit* white. *Habitat* in coniferous woodland. *Similar species R. mairei* is a beechwood species, with a softer flesh; inedible. *Edibility* inedible, and can cause vomiting when eaten raw.

GROUP Mushrooms and Toadstools
FAMILY Brittle-gills and Milk-caps (Russulaceae)

SEASON  **EDIBILITY** 

HABITAT  On the ground in woodlands or associated with trees

RUSSULA FRAGILIS
Fragile Russula

A delicate, purplish *Russula* species, with a grooved cap margin, and a peppery taste.

Cap ¾–2¼ in/2–6 cm in diameter, easily broken, convex to depressed, sticky when moist, purplish red or often much paler, with a grooved margin. *Gills* adnexed to adnate, white to pale cream, with an uneven edge. *Stem* ¾–2¾ × 3⁄16–⅜ in/2–7 × 0.5–1 cm, white, solid, slightly swollen towards the base. *Flesh* brittle, pure white, with a faint fruity odour. *Spore deposit* white. *Habitat* grows commonly in all kinds of woodland. *Similar species R. aquosa* is larger, with a pinkish violet cap, growing in oak woodland, while *R. betularum* is small, pale pink, and grows under birch trees; both inedible. *Edibility* inedible, because of the very acrid taste.

GROUP Mushrooms and Toadstools
FAMILY Brittle-gills and Milk-caps (Russulaceae)

SEASON  **EDIBILITY** 

HABITAT  On the ground in woodlands or associated with trees

RUSSULA NIGRICANS
Blackening Russula

Very common and the largest of the brittle-gills (*Russula* species); recognized by the widely spaced gills and blackening flesh.

Cap 4–8 in/10–20 cm in diameter, convex then becoming depressed, fleshy, at first white but soon discolouring dark brown to black, dry. *Gills* adnate, pinkish yellow, finally blackening, very thick and widely spaced. *Stem* 1¼–3 × ⅜–1¼ in/3–8 × 1–3 cm, short and stocky, white then blackening similarly to the cap. *Flesh* thick, white becoming blood-red then black, with a fruity smell. *Spore deposit* white. *Habitat* under various species of trees, often beech. *Similar species R. adusta* differs in having crowded gills; inedible. *Edibility* poor.

GROUP Mushrooms and Toadstools
FAMILY Brittle-gills and Milk-caps (Russulaceae)

SEASON 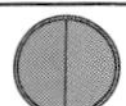 **EDIBILITY** 

HABITAT  On the ground in woodlands or associated with trees

RUSSULA VIRESCENS
Cracked Green Russula

An uncommon species of deciduous woods, recognized by the green cap which has the surface cracking.

Cap 2¾–4¾ in/7–12 cm in diameter, green or yellowish green, convex, expanding and often depressed at centre, the cuticle towards the margin cracking to give a scaly appearance. *Gills* almost free, crowded, narrow, white. *Stem* 1½–3½ × ¾–1½ in/4–9 × 2–4 cm, whitish, usually tapered, powdered above, otherwise smooth. *Flesh* white, with no distinctive smell, and mild taste. *Spore deposit* cream. *Habitat* in deciduous woods, often with beech. *Similar species* in North America, *R. crustosa* has a more greyish yellow cap, and an ochre spore deposit. *R. aeruginosa, R. heterophylla* and *R. cyanoxantha* var. *pelteraui* are greenish, but lack cracking of the cap surface. All are edible. *Edibility* a good edible species.

GROUP Mushrooms and Toadstools
FAMILY Brittle-gills and Milk-caps (Russulaceae)

SEASON  **EDIBILITY** 

HABITAT  On the ground in woodlands or associated with trees

SCHIZOPHYLLUM COMMUNE

Split Gill

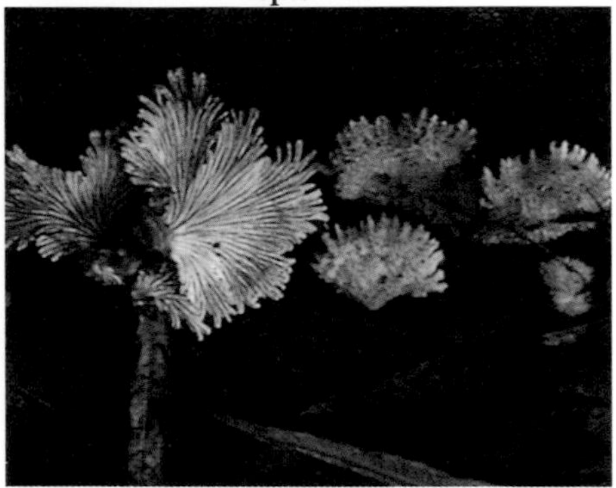

A common species of warmer regions, forming tiers of small, grey, hairy brackets on stumps and trunks.

Cap 3/8–1½ in/1–4 cm in diameter, shell-shaped and laterally attached, pale grey or pure white in very dry conditions, densely hairy-scaly. *Gills* radiating from a lateral attachment point, appearing to split lengthwise along their edges in dry weather and the sides curling upwards, narrow, grey. *Stem* none. *Flesh* thin, grey, leathery. *Spore deposit* white. *Habitat* on dead branches of deciduous trees, especially beech, also on domestic wood. *Similar species* the splitting gills and the tough, leathery texture separate this species from all other oyster mushrooms. *Edibility* inedible, too tough.

GROUP Mushrooms and Toadstools
FAMILY Split-gill (Schizophyllaceae)

SEASON 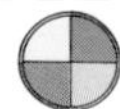 **EDIBILITY** 

HABITAT  On trees, stumps or woody debris

SCLERODERMA CITRINUM

Common Earthball *or* Pigskin Poison Puffball

A yellowish, species which lacks a stalk and has a thick, scaly wall.

Fruitbody 1½–4 in/4–10 cm across, subglobose, lacking a stalk, arising from white, string-like mycelium, yellowish or yellowish brown, the surface splitting into thick, conspicuous scales. *Wall* thick, breaking open irregularly at maturity to expose the spore mass. *Inner tissue* whitish at first, soon purplish black patterned with white veins, firm, with unpleasant smell, finally powdery when the spores are mature. *Habitat* on heaths and in open woodland, especially on sandy soil. *Similar species S. geaster* is similar, but is brown and opens by spreading star-like rays; inedible. *Edibility* inedible.

GROUP Puffballs and allies
FAMILY Earthball (Sclerodermataceae)

SEASON  **EDIBILITY** 

HABITAT  On the ground in woodlands or associated with trees

SCUTELLINIA SCUTELLATA

Eyelash Fungus *or* Eyelash Cup

Recognized by the gregarious, bright orange-red, disc-shaped fruitbodies which bear long, dark brown hairs at the margin.

Fruitbody ⅛–⅜ in/0.3–1 cm across, saucer-shaped, slightly concave, bearing stiff, dark brown tapered hairs up to 1⁄16 in/0.1 cm long on the outer surface, especially at the margin. *Fertile surface* bright orange-red, smooth. *Outer surface* pale brown. *Flesh* pale orange. *Habitat* gregarious on rotten wood or damp soil; common. *Similar species* other species of *Scutellinia* may be similar; many have shorter marginal hairs, but microscopic examination is required for certain identification. All species inedible. *Edibility* inedible.

GROUP Cup Fungi
FAMILY Eyelash Cup Fungi (Pyronemataceae)

SEASON 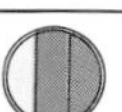 **EDIBILITY** 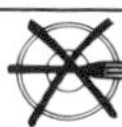

HABITAT  On trees, stumps or woody debris

SERPULA LACRYMANS

Dry Rot Fungus

The well-known, destructive fungus of domestic wood, characterized by fruitbodies with a rusty brown lower surface; spreading by greyish brown, fibrous cords.

Fruitbody spreading over the substrate and forming large, pancake-like patches, up to ⅜ in/1 cm thick, eventually the margin curving to form indefinite brackets. *Upper surface* white to cream-coloured, bruising brownish, with a broad, white margin. *Lower surface* strongly wrinkled and folded to irregularly pore-like, olive-brown to deep rusty brown. *Flesh* white, tough, fibrous, with a pungent odour. *Spore deposit* yellowish brown. *Habitat* on domestic conifer wood found in damp, poorly ventilated buildings. *Similar species S. himantioides* grows on forest conifers and is much thinner in appearance; inedible. *Edibility* inedible.

GROUP Bracket Fungi
FAMILY Dry and Wet Rot (Coniophoraceae)

SEASON  **EDIBILITY** 

HABITAT  On trees, stumps or woody debris

SPARASSIS CRISPA
Cauliflower Fungus

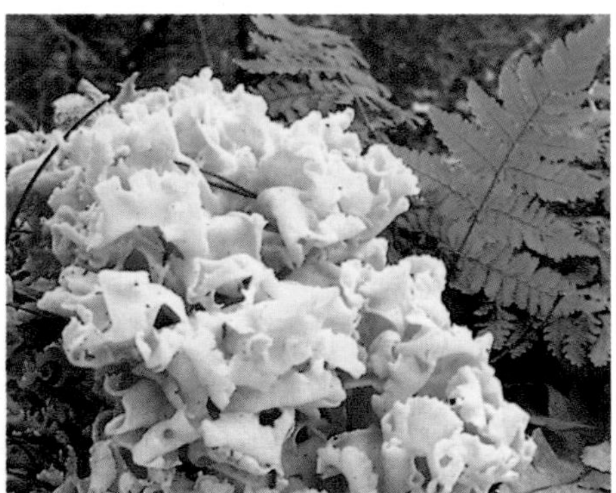

A large fungus, resembling a cauliflower. *Fruitbody* 4–16 in/10–40 cm in diameter, whitish to cream finally brownish, with numerous, flat, ribbon-like branches, 3/8–3/4 in/1–2 cm broad, wavy and leaf-like; arising from a stalk-like base, 3/4–3 × 1 1/4–1 1/2 in/2–8 × 3–4 cm, solid. *Flesh* white, thin, tough, with a sweetish odour. *Spore deposit* cream coloured. *Habitat* at base of conifer-stumps, especially pine. *Similar species S. laminosa* is less branched and usually grows with either beech or oak; edible. *Edibility* edible and good.

GROUP Club Fungi
FAMILY Cauliflower Fungus (Sparassidaceae)

SEASON  **EDIBILITY** 

HABITAT  On trees, stumps or woody debris

STEREUM HIRSUTUM
Yellow Stereum

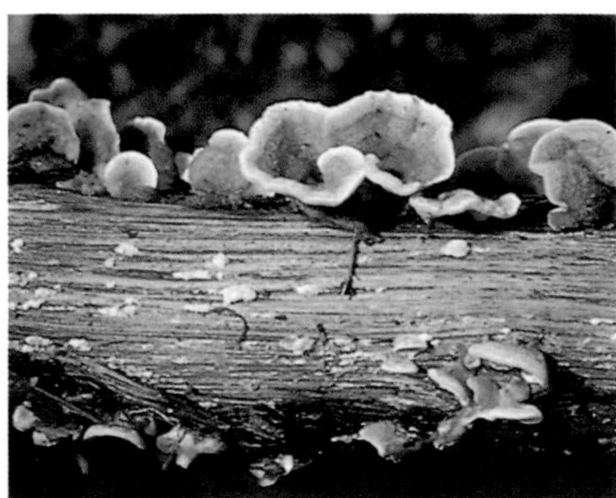

The most common *Stereum* species, forming many yellowish brackets.

Cap 3/4–2 1/4 in/2–6 cm in diameter, bracket-like, with the broad basal attachment region spreading over the substrate. *Upper surface* yellowish orange to greyish white, hairy but less so when old, with conspicuous concentric zoning, and a thin, wavy margin. *Lower surface* smooth, yellowish to brownish orange, not bruising reddish. *Flesh* 1/16 in/0.1–0.2 cm thick, yellowish, leathery-tough. *Spore deposit* white. *Habitat* on dead wood of deciduous trees. *Similar species S. subtomentosum* has a bright yellow margin, and grows on willow and alder; inedible. *S. insignitum* has brown zoning and grows on beech; inedible. *Coriolus versicolor* can look very similar but has white pores on the lower surface; inedible. *Edibility* inedible

GROUP Bracket fungi
FAMILY Crust Fungus (Stereaceae)

SEASON 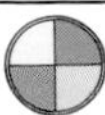 **EDIBILITY** 

HABITAT  On trees, stumps or woody debris

STROBILOMYCES STROBILACEUS
Old Man of the Woods

A very distinctive species with grey-brown colours, scaly cap, and flesh becoming reddish when cut.

Cap 3–8 in/8–20 cm across, hemispherical, expanding somewhat, covered with large, woolly, grey-brown or mouse-grey scales, margin shaggy with tooth-like remains of the veil. *Tubes* whitish or pale grey, reddening when cut; *pores* rather large, angular, greyish. *Stem* 2¾–4¾ × ⅝–1 in/7–12 × 1.5–2.5 cm, cylindrical, similarly coloured to the cap, paler above, somewhat scaly, bearing a shaggy ring. *Flesh* pale greyish, becoming reddish and finally greyish black when cut. *Spore deposit* violaceous black. *Habitat* in mixed woodland, especially in mature beech woods, also with oak and pine. *Similar species* unlikely to be confused with other species. *Edibility* edible but worthless.

GROUP Boletes
FAMILY Boletus (Boletaceae)

SEASON  **EDIBILITY** 

HABITAT  On the ground in woodlands or associated with trees

STROPHARIA AERUGINOSA
Verdigris Agaric *or* Green Stropharia

A common toadstool having, when young and fresh, a slimy, deep blue-green cap with white scales at the margin.

Cap 1¼–3 in/3–8 cm in diameter, conical or convex at first, becoming flattened, often with a raised centre, very slimy, greenish blue when young, with small white scales especially near the margin, the colour fading to pale yellowish with age. *Gills* adnate, at first white then purplish clay-brown, with white edges. *Stem* 1½–4 × ⅛–⅜ in/4–10 × 0.41–1 cm, cylindrical, slightly thickened at the base, hollow, white or pale green, slimy, bearing a scaly membranous ring below. *Flesh* whitish, usually with a green tint in the stem. *Spore deposit* purplish brown. *Habitat* in mixed woodland. *Similar species S. caerulea* has a scanty veil, while *S. albocyanea* is paler; both poisonous. *Edibility* **poisonous.**

GROUP Mushrooms and Toadstools
FAMILY Stropharia (Strophariaceae)

SEASON  **EDIBILITY** 

HABITAT  On the ground in woodlands or associated with trees

STROPHARIA SEMIGLOBATA
Dung Roundhead *or* Round Stropharia

A distinctive species recognized by the yellowish, hemispherical, slimy cap, thin ring on stem, and habitat.

Cap 3/8–1½ in/1–4 cm across, hemispherical, rarely expanding, pale yellow or straw coloured, slimy, smooth. *Stem* 1¼–4 × 1/16–3/16 in/3–10 × 0.2–0.4 cm, cylindrical, slightly bulbous at the base, whitish or pale yellowish, bearing a thin, fragile ring which is often incomplete or lost. *Gills* adnate, broad, purplish brown later blackish. *Flesh* pale, thin, without a distinctive smell. *Spore deposit* purplish brown. *Habitat* on dung of herbivores, especially horse and cattle, common. *Similar species* unlikely to be confused with other species. *Edibility* inedible.

GROUP Mushrooms and Toadstools
FAMILY Stropharia (Strophariaceae)

SEASON  **EDIBILITY** 

HABITAT  On dung or enriched soil

TARZETTA CUPULARIS
Elf Cup

A cup-shaped, short-stalked, greyish buff species growing on damp soil in woodland.

Fruitbody 3/8–3/4 in/1–2 cm across, remaining deeply cup-shaped, short stalked, margin with small, irregular teeth. *Inner surface* pale buff, with greyish tinge, smooth. *Outer surface* similarly coloured but paler, finely but distinctly scurfy. *Stem* short, cylindrical, partly buried. *Flesh* thin, brittle. *Habitat* on damp soil, in woods or at path edges, solitary or gregarious. *Similar species T. catinus* is larger, lacks greyish tints and has a shorter stalk; inedible. *Edibility* inedible.

GROUP Cup Fungi
FAMILY Large Cup Fungi (Pezizaceae)

SEASON 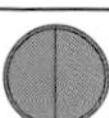 **EDIBILITY** 

HABITAT  On the ground in woodlands or associated with trees

THELEPHORA TERRESTRIS

Earth Fan *or* Common Fibre Vase

Commonly found in groups, among fallen conifer needles.

Fruitbody forming rosette-like clusters, sometimes more upright and vase-shaped, ¾–2¼ in/2–6 cm in diameter, consisting of several fan-shaped lobes with an irregular thin margin; upper surface greyish brown or darker, radially fibrous to scaly, with indistinct zoning; lower surface smooth or wrinkled, cocoa-brown. *Flesh* thin, tough and leathery, fibrous, with an earthy odour. *Spore deposit* cocoa-brown. *Habitat* on the ground, in coniferous woodland. *Similar species T. anthocephala* has erect, narrow branches, often with a whitish margin; inedible. *Edibility* inedible.

GROUP Bracket Fungi
FAMILY Earth Fan (Thelephoraceae)

SEASON 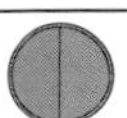 **EDIBILITY** 

HABITAT  On the ground in woodlands or associated with trees

TREMELLA MESENTERICA

Yellow Brain Fungus *or* Witches' Butter

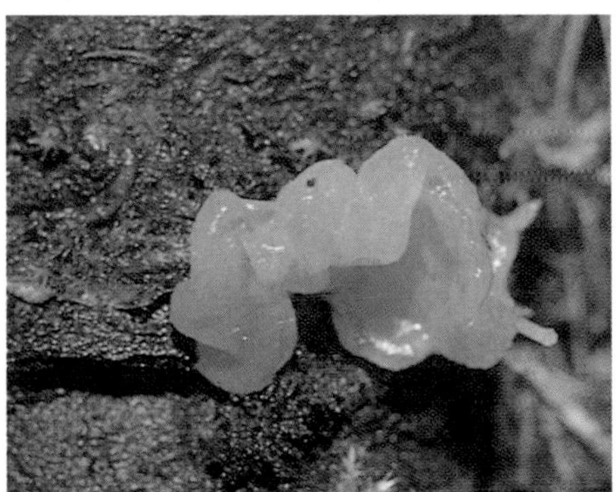

A distinctive species recognized by the orange-yellow colour, gelatinous flesh and irregular, brain-like shape.

Fruitbody ⅜–3 in/1–8 cm across, bright orange-yellow, irregular in shape, folded and lobed, softly gelatinous throughout, drying dark orange and horny. *Fertile surface* continuous. *Spore deposit* white. *Habitat* on dead branches of deciduous trees; common. *Similar species* unlikely to be confused with other species. *Edibility* inedible.

GROUP Jelly Fungus
FAMILY Yellow Brain Fungus (Tremellaceae)

SEASON 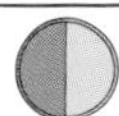 **EDIBILITY** 

HABITAT  On trees, stumps or woody debris

TRICHOGLOSSUM HIRSUTUM

Hairy Earth Tongue

An erect, club-shaped species distinguished by the velvety surface of the fruitbody.

Fruitbody 1¼–3 in/3–8 cm high, black or blackish brown, velvety throughout due to minute, stiff, blackish hairs, variable in shape, narrowly club-shaped or sometimes capitate, upper fertile part ⅛–¼ in/0.3–0.6 cm wide, laterally compressed, irregularly furrowed, sharply delimited from the stem. *Stem* up to 2¼ in/6 cm high, ⅛ in/0.2–0.4 cm wide, slightly compressed and sometimes furrowed. *Flesh* dark brown. *Habitat* usually in wet acid grassland, often among *Sphagnum* moss. *Similar species* other species of *Trichoglossum* can be distinguished only by microscopic examination. Species of *Geoglossum* are similar in shape and colour, but lack the velvety surface. *Edibility* edible.

GROUP Cup Fungi
FAMILY Earth Tongue (Geoglossaceae)

SEASON  **EDIBILITY** 

HABITAT  On the ground in grassland or open spaces

TRICHOLOMA FULVUM

Yellow-Brown Tricholoma

One of several brown *Tricholoma* species, recognized by the slimy cap and yellowish gills and flesh.

Cap 2¾–4¾ in/7–12 cm in diameter, convex to depressed, reddish brown and radially streaked, sticky. *Gills* sinuate, pale yellow soon developing reddish brown spots, crowded. *Stem* 2¾–4¾ × 3/16–⅜ in/7–12 × 0.5–1 cm, stocky, reddish brown, at first slimy, scaly below. *Flesh* white, yellow in stem, with a smell of rancid meal. *Spore deposit* white. *Habitat* especially coniferous and birch woods. *Similar species T. albobrunneum* has a dark brown cap and white gills; inedible. *Edibility* inedible.

GROUP Mushrooms and Toadstools
FAMILY Tricholoma (Tricholomataceae)

SEASON  **EDIBILITY** 

HABITAT  On the ground in woodlands or associated with trees

TRICHOLOMOPSIS DECORA
Decorated Mop

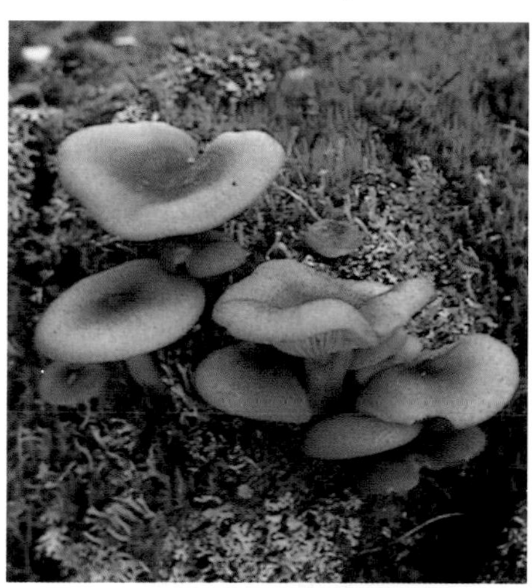

A species of mountainous regions.

Cap 1¼–3 in/3–8 cm in diameter, convex becoming depressed in the centre, pale yellowish orange, with tiny, blackish brown, scales over the surface. *Gills* adnexed, yellow, narrow and crowded. *Stem* 1¼–2¼ × 3/16–3/8 in/3–6 × 0.5–1 cm, cylindrical, yellow, with darker scales. *Flesh* whitish, thick. *Spore deposit* white. *Habitat* on dead wood of coniferous trees. *Similar species T. rutilans* has purplish tints, while *T. sulphuroides* is paler yellow with dark radiating streaking; both inedible. *Edibility* inedible.

GROUP Mushrooms and Toadstools
FAMILY Tricholoma (Tricholomataceae)

SEASON  **EDIBILITY** 

HABITAT  On trees, stumps or woody debris

VERPA CONICA
Smooth Thimble Cap

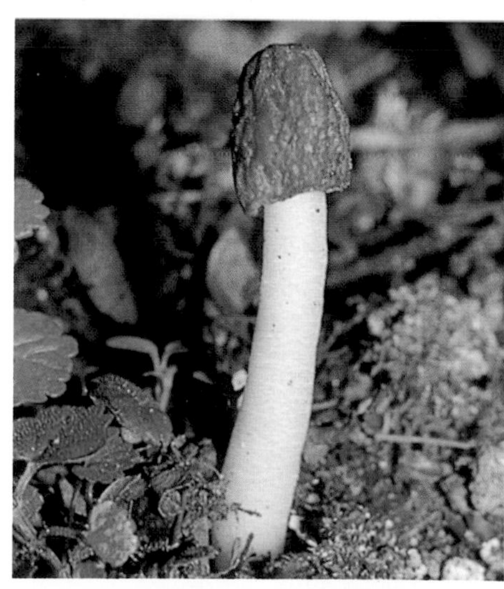

A distinctive species, with a brown, thimble-shaped cap and whitish stem.

Cap 5/8–1½ in/1.5–4 cm high, 3/8–¾ in/1–2 cm wide, bell- or thimble-shaped, dark- or olive-brown, wrinkled or furrowed, smooth, pendulous, attached only at the top of the stem. *Stem* 1¼–3 × ¼–3/8 in/3–8 × 0.6–1 cm, cylindrical, whitish or cream, with irregular bands of slightly darker granules, hollow. *Flesh* thin, brittle. *Habitat* among scrub, at roadsides, often on chalky soil. *Similar species V. bohemica* wrinkled cap; inedible. *Edibility* edible when cooked, poor.

GROUP Cup Fungi
FAMILY Morel (Morchellaceae)

SEASON  **EDIBILITY** 

HABITAT  On the ground in woodlands or associated with trees

VOLVARIELLA SPECIOSA

Rose-Gilled Grisette *or* Smooth Volvariella

A tall, solitary, pale mushroom with pink gills and a sac-like volva.

Cap 2¾–5½ in/7–14 cm in diameter, conical to convex, finally becoming flattened, whitish with a pale greyish brown centre, smooth, slimy when moist. *Gills* free, at first white gradually becoming pink, thin, broad, and very crowded. *Stem* 3½–7 × ⅜–⅝ in/9–18 × 1–1.5 cm, tall and cylindrical, fragile, hollow, whitish, with fine, brownish streaks; arising from a sac-like, white volva, which soon collapses. *Flesh* thin, soft and soon decaying. *Spore deposit* salmon-pink. *Habitat* growing on compost heaps, and richly manured soil. *Similar species* pink-gilled *Pluteus* species (edible, but worthless) lack a volva, while the poisonous *Amanita* species have white gills.*Edibility* said to be edible but great care must be taken to avoid confusion.

GROUP Mushrooms and Toadstools
FAMILY Pluteus (Pluteaceae)

SEASON  **EDIBILITY** 

HABITAT  On dung or enriched soil

XEROCOMUS CHRYSENTERON

Red-Cracked Boletus

A common but variable bolete; the velvety cap with reddish cracks and the yellow pores are distinctive.

Cap 1½–3 in/4–8 cm in diameter, convex to flat, dry, olive-brown to reddish brown, velvety when young, cracking to reveal underlying red flesh. *Tubes* slightly depressed around the stem apex, bright yellow but slowly discolouring blue-green; *pores* angular, bright yellow, staining greenish. *Stem* 1½–3 × 3/16–⅝ in/4–8 × 0.5–1.5 cm, slender, scurfy, yellowish with pinkish red tints, solid. *Flesh* thick, white to yellowish, slowly discolouring blue when broken. *Spore deposit* cinnamon-brown. *Habitat* in deciduous woodland, especially under oak trees. *Similar species X. subtomentosus* is very similar but lacks the red cracking on the cap surface; edible. *Edibility* edible but not recommended.

GROUP Boletes
FAMILY Xerocomus (Xerocomaceae)

SEASON  **EDIBILITY** 

HABITAT  On the ground in woodlands or associated with trees

XYLARIA HYPOXYLON

Candle Snuff Fungus *or* Carbon Antlers

A common species recognized by the slender, usually branched fruitbodies.

Fruitbody ¾–3 in/2–8 cm high, ⅛–¼ in/0.3–0.6 cm across, erect, cylindrical to flattened, usually forked and antler-shaped, pointed, stalked; upper fertile portion at first white, powdery, later darkening, becoming black; sometimes unbranched. *Stalk* black, hairy. *Flesh* white, with a thin, black crust. *Spore deposit* black. *Habitat* on dead wood. *Similar species X. carpophila* is more slender and occurs on rotten beech mast in litter; inedible. *Edibility* inedible.

GROUP Flask Fungi
FAMILY Candle Snuff (Xylariaceae)

SEASON 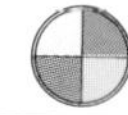 **EDIBILITY** 

HABITAT  On trees, stumps or woody debris

XYLARIA POLYMORPHA

Dead Man's Fingers

A large, black, club-shaped species which grows in clusters on dead stumps.

Fruitbody 1¼–4 in/3–10 cm high, ⅜–1¼ in/1–3 cm across, black, variable in form, irregularly club-shaped, sometimes lobed, with a short, cylindrical stalk; surface of fertile part minutely papillate, granular. *Flesh* white, with a thin black crust in which the fertile, flask-shaped structures (perithecia) are embedded. *Spore deposit* black. *Habitat* in clusters on dead stumps, especially of beech. *Similar species X. longipes* is more slender, less clustered and occurs on roots and branches of sycamore and other species of *Acer*; inedible. *Edibility* inedible.

GROUP Flask Fungi
FAMILY Candle Snuff (Xylariaceae)

SEASON 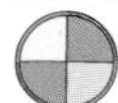 **EDIBILITY** 

HABITAT  On trees, stumps or woody debris

INDEX OF COMMON NAMES

Alcohol ink-cap 23
Amethyst deceiver 39
Angel's wings 62
Anise-scented clitocybe 19
Artist's fungus 32

Beefsteak fungus 30
Big laughing gymnopilus 33
Birch polypore 61
Black morel 51
Black trumpet 26
Blackening russula 69
Bladder cap 58
Bleeding mycena 53
Blood-red cortinarius 29
Blood-stained bracket 28
Blue-green clitocybe 19
Blue-toothed leptonia 46
Bracelet cortinarius 26
Broad-gilled agaric 50
Brown birch bolete 43
Brown cone cap 22
Brown funnel polypore 21
Brown roll-rim 58
Buff meadow cap 16

Candle snuff fungus 79
Carbon antlers 79
Carbon balls 29
Cauliflower fungus 72
Cellar fungus 22
Cep 14
Changeable melanoleuca 51
Changing pholiota 39
Chanterelle 17
Charcoal pholiota 61
Chicken of the woods 42
Cinnabar-red polypore 66
Citron amanita 12
Clustered psathyrella 65
Collared earthstar 32
Common earthball 70
Common fibre vase 75
Common ink-cap 23
Common morel 52
Common puffball 47
Common scabre stalk 43
Common stinkhorn 60
Common white helvella 35
Common white inocybe 38
Conical wax cap 36
Cracked green russula 69
Cramp balls 29
Crested coral fungus 18
Crust-like cup 67

Dead man's fingers 79
Death cap 13
Deceiver 40
Decorated mop 77
Dry rot fungus 71
Dryad's saddle 64
Dung roundhead 74
Dusty puffball 15
Dye polypore 59

Early cup fungus 58
Earth fan 75
Elf cup 74
Emetic russula 68
Eyelash cup 71
Eyelash fungus 71

Fairy cake hebeloma 35
Fairy ring champignon 49
False chanterelle 37
False death cap 12
False morel 34
Fawn pluteus 63
Field mushroom 9
Fluted white helvella 35
Fly agaric 12
Fragile russula 68
Freckle-gilled gymnopilus 34

Gem-studded puffball 47
Giant club 18
Giant puffball 42
Girolle 17
Golden false pholiota 59
Golden pholiota 60
Golden spindles 19
Golden-thread cordyceps 25
Greasy tough shank 20
Green stropharia 73
Green-spored lepiota 17
Gregarious elf cup 53
Grey mottle-gill 57
Grooved bird's nest fungus 27
Gypsy mushroom 67

Hairy earth tongue 76
Half free morel 52
Honey fungus 13
Horn of plenty 26
Horse mushroom 8

Jelly antler fungus 15
Jelly babies 44
Jelly crepidotus 27
Jew's ear 14

King Alfred's cakes 29

Large pine polyporus 59
Lawyer's wig 23
Lemon peel fungus 56
Liberty cap 65
Lilac mycena 54
Little wheel toadstool 50
Luminescent panellus 57

Malodorous lepiota 44
Miller mushroom 20

Nitrous mycena 54
Non-inky coprinus 24

Ochre jelly club 44
Old man of the woods 73
Onion-stalked lepiota 47
Orange peel fungus 11
Orange pholiota 33
Oyster mushroom 63

Parasol mushroom 48
Parrot toadstool 36
Peaked inocybe 38
Pear-shaped puffball 48
Penny bun boletus 14
Pestle-shaped coral 18
Pick-a-back toadstool 55
Pig's ear gomphus 33
Pigskin poison puffball 70
Pine fire fungus 67
Pink mycena 54
Pink-fringed milk-cap 41
Pinwheel marasmius 50
Platterful mushroom 50
Poison paxillus 58
Poison pie 35
Prince 8
Pungent cystoderma 28

Razor-strop fungus 61
Red-banded cortinarius 26
Red-cracked boletus 78
Red-hot milk-cap 41
Red-rimmed bracket 31
Rooting shank 56
Rose-gilled grisette 78
Round stropharia 74
Rufous milk-cap 41

Saffron milk-cap 40
Saffron parasol 28
Salmon wax cap 16
Saw gilled leptonia 46
Scaly lentinus 43
Scaly wood mushroom 9
Scarlet caterpillar fungus 24

Shaggy ink-cap 23
Shaggy parasol 49
Sheep polypore 11
Silky nolanea 55
Slender psathyrella 64
Slender truffle cup 25
Smooth lepiota 46
Smooth thimble cap 77
Smooth volvariella 78
Soft slipper toadstool 27
Splash cups 27

Split gill 70
Spotted tough shank 21
Spring agaric 10
St George's mushroom 16
Stinking parasol 44
Straw-coloured fibre head 38
Stump puffball 48
Styptic fungus 57
Sulphur polypore 42
Sulphur tuft 37
Sweetbread mushroom 20

Tawny funnel cap 45
Thin-maze flat polypore 28
Tinder fungus 31
Tree ear 14
Trooping cordyceps 24
Trooping crumble caps 24
Turban fungus 34
Turkey-tail 25
Two-tone pholiota 39

Varicoloured bracket 25
Veiled oyster 62
Velvet shank 30
Verdigris agaric 73

Watery hypholoma 65
Wet rot fungus 22
White fibre head 38
Witch's hat 36
Witches' butter 75
Wood blewit 45
Woolly milk-cap 41

Yellow brain fungus 75
Yellow morel 52
Yellow stereum 72
Yellow tuning fork 15
Yellow-brown tricoloma 76
Yellow-foot agaricus 10
Yellow-staining mushroom 10
Yellow-tipped coral fungus 66